Scientific Perspectives on Animal Welfare

Edited by

W. Jean Dodds

Division of Laboratories and Research
New York State Department of Health
Albany, New York

F. Barbara Orlans

National Institutes of Health
Bethesda, Maryland

1982

ACADEMIC PRESS

A Subsidiary of Harcourt Brace Jovanovich, Publishers

New York   London
Paris   San Diego   San Francisco   São Paulo   Sydney   Tokyo   Toronto

ACADEMIC PRESS, INC.
111 Fifth Avenue, New York, New York 10003

United Kingdom Edition published by
ACADEMIC PRESS, INC. (LONDON) LTD.
24/28 Oval Road, London NW1   7DX

Library of Congress Cataloging in Publication Data
Main entry under title:

Scientific perspectives on animal welfare.

    Proceedings of the First Conference on Scientific
Perspectives in Animal Welfare, held Nov. 11-13,
1981, in Chevy Chase, Md., sponsored by the
Scientists Center for Animal Welfare.
    1. Animals, Treatment of--Congresses.
2. Animal experimentation--Congresses. I. Dodds,
W. Jean. II. Orlans, F. Barbara. III. Conference
on Scientific Perspectives in Animal Welfare
(1st : 1981 : Chevy Chase, Md.) IV. Scientistis
Center for Animal Welfare.
HV4704.S34   1982   179'.4   82-24375
ISBN 0-12-219140-4

CONTENTS

OVERVIEW

SECTION I
INVESTIGATOR RESPONSIBILITIES
IN ANIMAL EXPERIMENTATION

SECTION II
INSTITUTIONAL RESPONSIBILITIES
IN ANIMAL EXPERIMENTATION

SECTION III
FUNDING AGENCY RESPONSIBILITIES
IN ANIMAL EXPERIMENTATION

SECTION IV
EDITORIAL RESPONSIBILITIES
IN ANIMAL EXPERIMENTATION

SECTION V
PUBLIC POLICY AND RECOMMENDATIONS

CONTRIBUTORS

Numbers in parentheses indicate the pages on which the authors' contributions begin.

Perrie M. Adams, Ph.D. (39), *Associate Professor, Department of Psychiatry and Behavioral Sciences, University of Texas Medical Branch, Galveston, Texas*

Henry J. Baker, D.V.M. (49), *Professor and Chairman, Department of Comparative Medicine, University of Alabama, Birmingham, Alabama*

Robert M. Berne, M.D. (103), *Chairman and Charles Slaughter Professor of Physiology, Department of Physiology, University of Virginia School of Medicine, Charlottesville, Virginia*

Craig A. DaRif, D.V.M. (49), *Associate Director, Experimental Animal Resources, Department of Comparative Medicine, University of Alabama, Birmingham, Alabama*

Carlos E. Eyzaguirre, M.D. (69), *Professor and Head, Department of Physiology, University of Utah College of Medicine, Salt Lake City, Utah*

James G. Fox, D.V.M., Ph.D. (59), *Director, Division of Comparative Medicine, Massachusetts Institute of Technology, Cambridge, Massachusetts*

Michael W. Fox, D.Sc., Ph.D., B. Vet. Med., M.R.C.V.S. (107), *Director, Institute for the Study of Animal Problems, Washington, D.C.*

Frank B. Golley, Ph.D. (95), *Research Professor of Ecology, Institute of Ecology, University of Georgia, Athens, Georgia*

Harlyn O. Halvorson, Ph.D. (109), *Director, Rosensteil Basic Medical Sciences Research Center, Brandeis University, Waltham, Massachusetts*

Frederick W. L. Kerr, M.D. (19), *Professor, Department of Neurologic Surgery, Mayo Foundation and Medical School, Rochester, Minnesota*

Keith Kraner, D.V.M. (83), *Executive Secretary, Surgery, Anesthesiology and Trauma Study Section, National Institutes of Health, Bethesda, Maryland*

J. Russell Lindsey, D.V.M. (49), *Professor, Department of Comparative Medicine, University of Alabama, Birmingham, Alabama*

Franklin M. Loew, D.V.M., Ph.D.[1] (3), *Director and Professor, Division of Comparative Medicine, The Johns Hopkins University School of Medicine, Baltimore, Maryland*

Thomas E. Malone, Ph.D. (7), *Acting Director, National Institutes of Health, Bethesda, Maryland*

Karl Johan Öbrink, M.D., Ph.D. (55), *Professor, Department of Physiology, Uppsala University, Uppsala, Sweden*

F. Barbara Orlans, Ph.D. (85), *Scientific Officer, National Heart, Lung, and Blood Institute, National Institutes of Health, Bethesda, Maryland*

David J. Ramsay, B.M., D.Phil. (77), *Professor, Department of Physiology, University of California School of Medicine, San Francisco, California*

Harry C. Rowsell, D.V.M., Ph.D. (43), *Executive Director, Canadian Council on Animal Care, and Professor, Department of Pathology, University of Ottawa, Ottawa, Ontario, Canada*

Richard C. Simmonds, D.V.M. (63), *Director, Department of Laboratory Animal Medicine, Uniformed Services University of the Health Sciences, Bethesda, Maryland*

Joseph S. Spinelli, D.V.M. (77) *Director, Animal Care Facility, University of California School of Medicine, San Francisco, California*

Garth J. Thomas, Ph.D. (101), *Professor, Center for Brain Research, University of Rochester Medical Center, Rochester, New York*

Marc E. Weksler, M.D. (33), *Wright Professor of Medicine, Division of Geriatrics and Gerontology, Department of Medicine, Cornell University Medical College, New York, New York*

---

[1]Present address: *Dean, School of Veterinary Medicine, Tufts University, Boston, Massachusetts.*

PREFACE

The papers, discussion, and recommendations contained in this book emanated from the First Conference on Scientific Perspectives in Animal Welfare sponsored by the Scientists Center for Animal Welfare. The meeting represented the beginning of a coordinated national effort by scientists to take the initiative for responsible use of animals in research.

Ninety scientists participated in the conference, and were from a variety of scientific backgrounds: from research institutions, universities, industrial laboratories, and some came as representatives from professional scientific associations. There were forty-four veterinarians, thirty-three research scientists with Ph.D. degrees, twelve physicians, and one dentist. Attendees came from areas throughout the United States as well as from Sweden, Australia, England, and Canada.

A few background comments are appropriate to describe the sponsoring organization, the Scientists Center for Animal Welfare. It is a nonprofit organization based in Washington, D.C. It was established in 1978 in response to a 1977 article written by Jeremy Stone, Director of the Federation of American Scientists.* He had called for the formation of an organization of scientists which would "adopt a balanced and undefensive attitude" regarding animal welfare. This would add luster to the scientific community, he stated.

A major objective of the Scientists Center is to help sensitize scientists to the issues involved in the humane treatment of animals. It stands on the general principle that all matters of public concern should be freely discussed, and that scientists themselves should take the initiative in establishing and maintaining a high credibility and accountability in matters of public conscience. This conference marked a major step in the realization of these goals.

The functions of the Center are to foster the humane stewardship of animals by educating scientists and the public about animal welfare; to promote intelligent and humane decisions in establishing public policy; to collect and exchange

*FAS Public Interest Report, *Special Issue: Animal Rights.* Federation of American Scientists, Washington, D.C., Vol., 30 #8, Oct. 1977, pp. 1–8.

scientific information relevant to animal welfare; and to encourage universities and professional schools to offer courses on the ethical aspects of our interrelationships with animals and on the technical skills involved in handling animals. A Board of Trustees—nine scientists representing a broad field of interests in biomedical research, agricultural science, and wildlife research—meet regularly to oversee the Center's activities.

Many individuals have contributed to the success of the conference. We would like to acknowledge the contributions of other members of our Board of Trustees, Richard Simmonds, Thomas Hartsock, Sherman Bloom, Bruce Feldmann, Michael W. Fox, Victor Scheffer, Jeremy Stone, and our two new Board members, Henry Baker and David Ramsay, for their service to the Scientists Center for Animal Welfare. Also, we thank Dr. Alan Levensohn of the New York State Department of Health for donating his time and suggestions in an editorial capacity and Ms. Marcia Feinleib of Prospect Associates for her organizing efforts and enthusiastic support of our endeavors.

W. Jean Dodds
Vice-President

F. Barbara Orlans
President

Scientists Center for
Animal Welfare

OVERVIEW

INTRODUCTION

Public concern about the humane use of animals in biomedical experimentation has been increasing steadily over the recent decades while animals have continued to play an indispensable role in scientific research. The papers comprising this book mark the first attempt by scientists to show that the advancement of science and of humane ethics are consonant and complementary.

Accountability of scientists for the proper use of animals in experimentation can be achieved by a series of review procedures that correspond to the four sections in the book. The first part discusses the role of the investigator who develops the idea and plans the experimental protocol. The second part involves the research institution which is responsible (primarily through its Animal Care Committee) for ensuring compliance with local, national, and Federal standards of animal welfare. The third part involves the funding agency. Here, the animal research protocols are reviewed and assessed for both scientific merit and humaneness of the experimental procedures. The fourth part is the publication of the completed work and includes editorial responsibility for review of the manuscripts, for adequate description of the experimental procedures, and for scientific merit.

Invited speakers at the conference addressed each of these topics and represented a wide range of scientific interests and viewpoints. They discussed current issues of concern, including the welfare of research animals, the feasibility of reducing the animals used or the invasiveness of the experimental procedure, and the economic and ethical costs of animals used in experimentation. Workshops were convened thereafter and addressed other issues or concerns, identified areas of special consideration, determined objectives, and elicited a series of important recommendations to serve as a guide to future directions the biomedical community might pursue. These recommendations are compiled at the end of the book. Discussions surrounding the recommendations are found in the papers and the workshop summaries.

In addition to these four parts, there are special chapters by Franklin Loew on the historical background of animal experimentation, by Harlyn Halvorson on public policy issues, and by Thomas Malone on the move toward perfecting policies and standards for animal welfare. The title of Dr. Malone's chapter is "Toward Refinement, Replacement, and Reduction in the Care and Use of Laboratory Animals." This title incorporates the three tenets of humane experimentation expounded by Russell and Burch in their classic text of 1959.[1] These three principles--refinement, replacement, and reduction--are commonly known as the three R's of research. Refinement means modifying existing techniques so that an experimental animal will experience less stress or pain. Replacement involves substituting non-animal procedures for animal experiments, thereby leading to reduction in numbers of animals used. Reduction involves seeking alternatives by any means that reduce ethical costs in terms of harm to animals. The most common means to achieve this is to lessen the invasiveness of the animal procedure.

Now, 20 years after the publication of Russell and Burch's text, the issues of humane animal experimentation are again addressed. The present volume will add a further step toward wider understanding of ways to achieve humaneness.

[1]Russell, W. M. S., and Burch, R. L. Principles of Humane Experimental Technique. Methuen, London (1959).

DEVELOPMENTS IN THE HISTORY OF THE USE OF ANIMALS IN MEDICAL RESEARCH

Franklin M. Loew[1]

Division of Comparative Medicine
The Johns Hopkins University
School of Medicine
Baltimore, Maryland

The earliest cited use of animals in medical research is that provided in the works by Galen (129–199 A.D.), the Greek medical scientist. The earliest known illustrations of what has come to be called vivisection are those showing Galen and his colleagues experimenting upon a live pig. More antecedents of the present use of animals can be traced to the anatomic dissections of people and animals in the 1500's and 1600's. Vesalius, for example, was one of the most important of the early anatomists; the first famous painting by Rembrandt, in 1632, is said to be "The Anatomical Lecture of Professor Tulp." There had been substantial resistance in clerical circles to anatomic dissections during the Middle Ages, which was attributed to a suspicion on the part of religious leaders that certain knowledge simply should not be obtained (7).

In 1791 Galvani published "On Electrical Forces in Muscular Motion," in which his now well-known experiments on the crural nerve in the frog's leg were illustrated. At about the same time Lavoisier, in France, was carrying out experiments on guinea pigs in which the relationship between the maintenance and generation of body heat and the oxygen in the air was being observed.

Probably the most frequently cited scientist in the progression of animal use in medical research is Claude Bernard of France, whose work An Introduction to Experimental

[1]Presently, Dean, School of Veterinary Medicine, Tufts University, Boston, Massachusetts.

SCIENTIFIC PERSPECTIVES ON ANIMAL WELFARE

3

Medicine is considered a classic. Bernard produced many important concepts and observations, not least of which was the idea that observation of the appropriate animal species is the key to making observations relevant to the human situation under study. That is, the entire experiment rests on the selection of the appropriate animal (5).

Bernard's countryman, Louis Pasteur, was also one of the earliest users of animals in research in today's sense, and he carried out elegant experiments on anthrax in sheep and rabies in dogs. Pasteur did not limit himself to mammals but studied also the diseases of silkworms. There is ample evidence that Pasteur felt uncomfortable with experiments on living animals, but he knew that at that time there was no other way to obtain the scientific information which was needed (4).

The mid-19th century was also a period of developments in neighboring Germany, where such scientists as Rudolph Virchow and Emil Behring were conducting animal experiments in experimental pathology and bacteriology. Robert Koch, whose name is associated with investigations into infectious diseases, was an avid investigator of the naturally occurring diseases of animals for the light which these might shed upon human disorders.

At the turn of the century, the Russian physiologist Ivan Pavlov carried out his famous experiments on the digestive system of the dog, which led to his description of the relationship between certain physiological responses and environmental stimuli, i.e., what has come to be known as the conditioned response. Perhaps no other phrase in the English language related to the use of animals in research has been used as much as "Pavlov's dog."

It was not surprising that by 1900 the value of the use of animals in medical research was well accepted by American society. Major strides had been made in the 30 years between 1870 and 1900 regarding the knowledge of specific infections, improvements in surgical technique, and the use of animals in teaching medical scientists. Advertisements regularly appeared in newspapers soliciting unwanted animals, particularly dogs or cats, for university teaching or research. The work of Darwin, however, raised--for some individuals, at least--disturbing questions about man's seemingly unfettered ability to carry out experiments on animals. In England particularly, organizations such as the RSPCA began to oppose most, if not all, animal use in science on the grounds that (a) if Darwin was correct, the pain felt by animals was undeniably similar to the pain felt by humans, and (b) inflicting such pain was undesirable at any cost. French's excellent book (2) has reviewed the subject extensively. In

the United States, SPCA's were formed in New York, Philadelphia, and Boston with similar concerns about, and sometimes objections to, animal use in medical science (6,8).

The period between 1900 and 1940 was marked by continued
use of animals in medical research, particularly in the areas
of surgery and physiology. By World War II animal use was an
accepted part of all medical research, and institutions such
as the Rockefeller Institute had made major investments in
facilities appropriate to their housing and care. After
World War II increases in animal use accompanied the major
increases in funding for research provided by the Federal
government, eventually through the National Institutes of
Health.

The development of laboratory animal science and medicine
in the United States, as a direct result of the use of animals in science, has recently been reviewed (1).

In 1959 and 1960, a new drug, thalidomide, was introduced
in Europe, and certain major birth defects in human infants
resulted from use of this drug during early gestation. Subsequent study revealed that the drug's effects were not
widely found in animal species. In the United States this
had the effect of requiring far more extensive animal testing
of drugs before marketing. No single event in recent history
has caused a greater use of animals than did the thalidomide
incident, although animal use in drug development and toxi-
cology can be differentiated from animal use in investigative
medical research (4).

With increasing animal use came increasing recognition by
both the public and the scientific community that guidelines,
if not laws, were required to ensure proper animal acquisition and use. Thus in 1963, the first edition of what has
come to be known as the Guide for the Care and Use of Laboratory Animals was published, and the U.S. Public Health
Service began to require all recipients of grants in which
animals were being used to adhere to the guidelines in that
document (1). In 1965-66, the 89th Congress held hearings on
animals in research, with an emphasis on the traffic in dogs
and cats intended to be used for research or experimentation.
These hearings led to the first national law in the United
States that dealt with animals in research. Initially called
the Laboratory Animal Welfare Act, it has been amended several times and is now known as the Animal Welfare Act, the
only such Federal law in the country. Annual statistics on
the use of certain species of animals in research and testing
in the United States are kept by the U.S. Department of
Agriculture, which has responsibility for administration of
the Animal Welfare Act.

The Institute of Laboratory Animal Resources, National
Academy of Sciences--National Research Council, has also

carried out studies to determine the numbers of animals used. A recent study indicates that there was an approximately 40 percent decrease in animal use between 1968 and 1978 in the United States (3). A similar trend has been reported in England. Thus animal use in medical research--which was so crucial to its early development, as well as to the establishment of basic concepts in many fields--seems to have declined sharply in the last 10 years. This is probably due to several factors, such as the high costs of acquiring and maintaining animals according to increasingly stringent guidelines and regulations, the increasingly greater amounts of space required for their maintenance, the fact that for testing (as opposed to investigative medical research) speedier and less expensive tests are being developed, and the fact that increasing public concern about certain types of animal use has resulted in pressure to cease such uses. On the other hand, the introduction of new concepts into biology has often had the effect of increasing animal use or changing the types of animal use. A recent example is the production of monoclonal antibodies, which requires the use of spleen cells.

REFERENCES

1. Cohen, B. J. (ed.), The origins of laboratory animal science and medicine, Lab. Anim. Sci. 30:737-800 (1980).
2. French, R. D., "Antivivisection and Medical Science in Victorian Society," 425 pp. Princeton University Press, Princeton (1975).
3. Institute of Laboratory Animal Resources, "National Survey of Laboratory Animal Facilities and Resources," 90 pp. NIH Pubication No. 80-2091, PHS/DHHS, Bethesda (1980).
4. Loew, F. M., Biomedical research and animal welfare: traditional viewpoints and future directions, Int. J. Stud. Anim. Prob. 2, 193-198 (1981).
5. Loew, F. M., Selection of experimental animal models, in "Measurement of Blood Flow" (D.N. Granger and G.B. Bulkley, eds.), pp. 47-55. Williams & Wilkins, Baltimore (1981).
6. Loew, F. M., Animal experimentation, Bull. Hist. Med. 56, 123-126 (1982).
7. Schwabe, C. W., "Cattle, Priests, and Progress in Medicine," 277 pp. University of Minnesota Press, Minneapolis (1978).
8. Turner, J., "Reckoning With the Beast," 190 pp. The Johns Hopkins University Press, Baltimore (1980).

TOWARD REFINEMENT, REPLACEMENT, AND REDUCTION IN THE CARE AND USE OF LABORATORY ANIMALS

Thomas E. Malone

Office of the Director
National Institutes of Health
Bethesda, Maryland

Those scientists who helped found the Scientists Center for Animal Welfare, establishing "a rapprochement between science and animal welfare," might have realized that its acronym, SCAW, is a word of Scandinavian origin meaning headland or promontory. A promontory is a high point of land or rock projecting into a body of water beyond the line of coast. It may also be a bluff or prominent hill overlooking or projecting into a lowland.

The contents of this book epitomize the meaning of SCAW, for it truly represents a high point in the evolution of policies regarding animal welfare. It is significant that scientists are moving away from the coastline of individual concern to aggregate action.

While we can be proud of the policies developed to date for the care and use of animals in research, the most important assurance comes from the positive and sensitive attitudes of research investigators and their coworkers in research. After all, they have the ultimate responsibility for the proper use of animals in experimentation. This sense of self-scrutiny and accountability is gratifying.

We live in a time marked by the ascending power of science and all that the biological revolution offers in the understanding of life processes and in bringing this new knowledge to bear on the alleviation of human disease. This is indeed a time for consensus building as we seek to adapt the principles for the care and use of animals to these exciting developments in science. It would be tragic if we did not resolve in our time the dilemma of the great 19th century French scientist Claude Bernard, the founder of modern experimental physiology. He had a domestic problem.

SCIENTIFIC PERSPECTIVES ON ANIMAL WELFARE

Madame Bernard was not only unsympathetic toward her hus-
band's work but succeeded in having their two daughters share
this hostility (1).   His wife and daughters were, in fact,
active and adamant antivivisectionists.   They begged him to
abandon research and to apply his energies toward a pros-
perous medical practice instead of tormenting helpless
animals in his laboratory.   Bernard continued his interests
in the "milieu interieur," and the sharp misunderstanding
with his family resulted in incompatibility and separation.
Historical accounts of Bernard's use of laboratory animals in
his research reveal that he did not meet, by any measure, the
standards we require today.   While his work was brilliant and
productive, it is unfortunate that he and his family could
not find a middle ground concerning the legitimate and appropriate care and use of animals in scientific endeavor.

Though more than a century has passed since Bernard's
many discoveries, we have not yet perfected our policies and
standards for animal welfare; we have not kept the public as
informed as they might be; and we have not taken all the
steps needed to make scientists more aware of their responsibilities toward laboratory animals.   Unlike the Bernard
family, we must find a middle but high ground that can accommodate legitimate scientific needs as well as animal welfare
concerns.   This imperative, in practical terms, is pushed by
strong Congressional interest in the subject, by nationwide
attention afforded those who have been accused of neglecting
animals used in laboratory research, and by those members of
the public who are either dedicated to the well-being of
animal subjects or opposed to any use of animals in research.

In this context, I would like to address several important issues and points, none of which will be unfamiliar.   I
want first to reaffirm the importance of laboratory animals
in the search for new knowledge and its application in the
prevention, treatment, and curing of human disease and in the
rehabilitation of those whose disabilities cannot be reversed
completely by modern medicine and surgery.   There is simply
no alternative to the use of animals for investigational
purposes.   There are areas in which animals can be partially
replaced by other biological or mathematical systems, but
these have limited applicability.

Virtually every major advance in health care stems in
whole or in part from research performed with animals.
Moreover, the application of new health care measures to
people before there has been sufficient animal experimentation sounds a counterpoint that cannot be ignored.   The
thalidomide tragedy is an example.   But the social imperative
for animal experimentation is not a license to take animals'
lives needlessly or to inflict pain and suffering that could

reasonably be avoided. Abuse of laboratory animals is as inconsistent with good science as it is with good conscience.

I need not dwell at length on the need for judicious involvement of animals for the advancement of biomedical knowledge. We are well aware of historical examples which have contributed indispensable insights to the corpus of medical information.

In the 17th century William Harvey examined and compared invertebrates, vertebrates, and mammals--dozens of species-- in order to develop an understanding of the cardiovascular circulatory system in the human. He said, "Had anatomists only been as conversant with the dissection of the lower animals as they are with that of the human body, the matters that have heretofore kept them in perplexity of doubt would, in my opinion, have made them free of every kind of dif- ficulty." Harvey laid the way for Reverend Stephen Hales some 80 years later to identify the rise and fall of blood in a glass tube connected to the crural artery, calling this "alternate systoles and diastoles." Today, while the root causes of hypertension still elude us, its pharmacological management is now possible, and we have witnessed in recent times a remarkable decrease in deaths from cardiovascular disease and stroke. This success story would not have been possible without three centuries of experimental work with animals.

The history of the struggle against infectious diseases reveals almost total dependence on (a) animals afflicted with the disease under study, and (b) the production, by means of animals, of viral vaccines. And this struggle has not only reduced disease among humans but has greatly benefited the health and well-being of animals as well. Our victory over the scourge of smallpox has been possible only because of Jenner's 19th-century work with the cow. The eradication of smallpox has been one of the most remarkably successful efforts of the World Health Organization, and we cannot help but reflect on the centuries of pain and suffering this disease brought to countless individuals throughout history.

During this century, research on atherosclerosis in chicks and the well-known testing of the polio vaccine in monkeys are further witnesses to the public's dependence on animal research for its medical well-being. More recently, hepatitis-B research with chimpanzees has produced a possible vaccine for this infectious disease; our progress in the study of leprosy has been enhanced through use of the arma- dillo, while neurophysiological studies on nonhuman primates have radically altered our understanding of the right and left halves of the brain and of image processing. This neurophysiological research resulted in Nobel Prizes for three American researchers.

Biological tests of various kinds play an indispensable role in the improvement of medical methods and the protection of human health and safety. The development of new drugs and the detection of toxic substances in the environment are two of many such examples. Historically, such testing has relied almost exclusively on techniques involving intact laboratory animals, usually rodents. Dogs, cats, and nonhuman primates have been used also, but in much smaller numbers. The objective in virtually every case has been to capitalize upon the physiological similarities between these animals and humans to identify effects that one might expect to find in human populations without actually putting humans at risk.

The enormous and continuing efforts to prevent, cure, and treat disease in humans and in animals require us to continue to use animals. Our use of animals directly reflects our recognition of the fact that we are biologically related to and ecologically dependent on other living organisms. Therefore, in respecting human beings, we must also show respect for all living things.

The second point I want to emphasize is that we must support efforts to replace animals in biological testing where feasible; to reduce their numbers in research and testing as far as possible, consistent with sound scientific design; and to refine their use in science in order to obtain the most efficient result with the least cost in animal resources.

As reported by Dr. William Raub in recent Congressional testimony, some progress is being made in the development of new techniques that might one day replace the use of intact animals in testing. Bacterial systems are being used to detect substances that might cause genetic damage and in the testing of potentially toxic substances. In like manner, nerve-cell cultures and invertebrates may be used to detect agents that cause abnormal development and to allow study of mechanisms causing abnormalities. Certainly recombinant DNA technology offers an unprecedented opportunity for the production and evaluation of diagnostic and therapeutic substances. But as we seek nonanimal testing methods, our hopes and expectations will have to be kept in tune with biological reality. As Dr. Raub observed, "The extraordinary complexity of living systems and our woefully incomplete understanding of them cannot help but attenuate our ambitions."

While that search is going on, there are some immediate steps that can be taken. Improved methods of husbandry, better training of animal care personnel, and standardization of research procedures and facilities will both prevent unnecessary involvement of animal subjects and improve the overall quality of our scientific efforts.

The merits of each of these approaches, together with the utilization of mathematical adjuncts for some types of bioassay procedures, were recently considered in a conference hosted by the National Institutes of Health (NIH) in cooperation with other agencies involved in toxicological testing. The importance of cooperation in this endeavor should not be underestimated. By pooling information, these agencies can reduce unnecessary repetition of experiments and avoid wasting precious animal resources.

Standardization in animal research is deserving of special mention. It means that proven feeding practices, husbandry methods, maintenance procedures, and safety standards for those who work in or near the laboratory should be included in the planning of each research proposal. By using animals of documented genetic background, the reliability of test results will be improved, and the need for larger, statistically acceptable test populations will be reduced.

Perhaps the most important standardization, however, must come in the education and selection of laboratory personnel. Animals, like humans, respond positively to those who are conscientious in their work and carry it out competently and completely. Research assistants responsible for routine care of laboratory animals must be as committed to their animal charges as the researcher is committed to the scientific knowledge he pursues.

Sound animal care practices, coupled with routine monitoring by animal care committees or by the American Association for the Accreditation of Laboratory Animal Care (AAALAC), will go far to assure the public that the responsible treatment of animals and economy in their use are consistent with that rigorous scientific method which provides the basis for medical knowledge on which we all depend.

I would finally like to comment on the efforts we have made to codify principles and practices governing the care and use of animals in research. In all probability, earliest man was a researcher of sorts, testing foods on animals to see if they were toxic or poisonous. Animal experiments are, in fact, recorded throughout history. Legal sanctions and guidelines are of relatively recent vintage--for this country, we find a prohibition against cruelty to animals in the first legal code of the Massachusetts Bay Colony--but it must be assumed that throughout history, as now, individual scientists have exercised self-discipline and governance in their own laboratories. This concern was finally reflected by the establishment of an Institute of Laboratory Animal Resources (ILAR) within the National Research Council in 1952. Its purpose was to disseminate information and educational materials in order to establish standards and upgrade laboratory animal resources.

In the very first formal grants policy statement issued by NIH in 1959, the care and treatment of animals was summarized as follows:

> It is expected that animals used in projects supported by the Public Health Service shall receive every consideration for their well-being; they shall be kindly treated, fed and watered properly, and their surroundings shall be maintained in a sanitary condition.

Under a contract from the NIH, ILAR in 1963 prepared a Guide for Laboratory Animal Facilities and Care, which has become a primary reference on standards of animal care. The guide was revised in 1965, 1968, 1972, and 1978, when it was republished under the title of Guide for the Care and Use of Laboratory Animals. Since its first issuance, more than a quarter of a million copies have been distributed.

An NIH policy which became effective January 1, 1979, requires each recipient institution of an NIH award to file with our Office for Protection from Research Risks (OPRR) a formally negotiated, written assurance regarding the care and use of laboratory animals. An acceptable assurance is a prerequisite for an award. Failure to comply with the assurance can result in significant penalties, including termination of an award, recovery of funds previously awarded, and ineligibility for further funding. In partial fulfillment of their obligations under these assurances, awardee institutions are required to be certified by a recognized accrediting organization, such as AAALAC, and/or to establish and operate a local animal care committee. Awardees also must agree to comply with applicable portions of the Animal Welfare Act, as well as State and local laws, if any.

The NIH traditionally has relied upon principal investigators and officials of awardee institutions to identify and correct problems as they arise. However, when particular aberrations come to our attention through such means as project site visits, other administrative interactions with awardees, or expressions of concern by members of the public, we make whatever inquiries seem indicated and follow up with whatever administrative actions seem appropriate.

We continue to believe that this basic approach is a cost-effective way to achieve a high degree of compliance with our laboratory animal guidelines without interfering unduly with the scope and pace of scientific inquiry. Nevertheless, we recognize that we have no fail-safe way to prevent occasional instances of real or apparent misuse or mistreatment of animals; and we take no solace from our belief that such instances are the exception, rather than the

rule.   We know we must do everything reasonable both to
achieve full compliance with our guidelines and to maintain
public confidence that such is the case.

The NIH is therefore prepared and committed to take
further steps to foster compliance with its own guidelines
and with the regulations of the U.S. Department of Agriculture.   We have come to this realization because experience
over the years, sparked by some unfortunate cases of mal-
treatment of animals, has made it clear that there are some
inadequacies in our policies and procedures.   I must also
note that among the powerful and dedicated stimulants for
change has been the President of SCAW, Dr. Barbara Orlans,
who keeps constantly before me and others at NIH and the
Congress, suggestions required to improve our system.   She
represents our viewpoint.

Some initial plans and ideas are as follows:

o   During the next year, we plan to initiate a program of
    site visits to selected awardee institutions to assess the
    adequacy of animal facilities and animal care practices.
    Some institutions would be visited on the basis of knowl-
    edge about real or potential problems, while others would
    be selected at random.   From these visits we hope to gain
    firsthand information that will lead to appropriate
    changes in our policies.

o   A key element in determining adherence to standards of use
    of laboratory animals is the review system that occurs
    first at the local institutional level and subsequently at
    NIH during the peer review process.   A primary goal of the
    planned site visits is to ascertain how well institutional
    animal care review committees work.   While we believe that
    most committees are functioning well, Dr. Orlans has posed
    for us some critical questions: "Are they paper commit-
    tees?   Are meetings held infrequently, and are they
    cursory in nature?   Is there conflict of interest in
    membership?   Does committee membership represent the broad
    interests of scientists, ethicists, and the public?   Are
    records poorly kept?   Does the committee review over time
    the experiments in progress?"   We will give attention to
    these questions and others.   For the immediate future we
    will examine the composition of animal care committees and
    require broader representation.

o   During the review of research protocols at NIH, attention
    is given to a number of critical questions, such as:

    Is this experiment worth doing?   That is, is it both
    meritorious and relevant to improving human health?

Are animals required to test this hypothesis? If so, has the proper species been selected and does the experimental design evince appropriate attention to limiting the number of animals involved?

Does the envisioned experimental procedure indicate that all reasonable precautions will be taken to prevent undue suffering by animals?

The NIH expects applicant investigators and institutional officials, peer review group members, and its own staff to be sensitive continually to these and related questions and to screen out inappropriate protocols, defective experimental designs, and other inadequately justified research plans. We believe our efforts in this area have been consistently effective. In order to assure that adequate attention is given to these aspects in the future, we plan to improve the documentation requirements associated with the review of research applications and ongoing research and to make certain that our key policies have indeed been complied with. Dr. Orlans has suggested that we might follow the system used by the Veterans Administration, and we are now determining if this would be appropriate for NIH.

o   It is not enough to distribute pamphlets and guidelines and expect that everyone will understand and follow them. We need to improve our educational and orientation efforts for applicants, grantees, members of local review boards, university officials, NIH advisory committee members, and NIH staff. By whatever process is most feasible--workshops, training courses, etc.--the appropriate NIH staff will be asked to develop a plan of action.

o   We have not made the strongest possible effort to educate and inform the public either about progress in science or about policies designed to protect animals in research. The scientific imperative is no longer autonomous, and we are, rightfully so, subject to continuous public scrutiny of the new legal, ethical, and social issues attending the biological revolution. Our staff will be asked to implement additional educational activities focused on the public.

o   Finally, we must address the important question of where we can obtain the necessary resources to upgrade animal care facilities and to provide the personnel and other support needed to assure compliance with existing and new policies. In this period of austerity, there are no easy answers. This area will continue to receive our attention.

The SCAW is to be commended for demonstrating its sure assumption of responsibilities for the proper use and care of animals in research. The benefits are far-reaching, and the social imperative for animal experimentation makes us <u>all</u> responsible for animal care, in and out of the laboratory. We will find, as we have in the past, that high-quality treatment of laboratory animals is as consistent with good research as it is with a good conscience.

REFERENCE

1. French, R.D., "Antivivisection and Medical Science in Victorian Society," 425 pp. Princeton University Press, Princeton (1975).

SECTION 1

INVESTIGATOR RESPONSIBILITIES
IN ANIMAL EXPERIMENTATION

THE INVESTIGATOR'S RESPONSIBILITIES
IN RESEARCH USING ANIMALS

Frederick W. L. Kerr

Department of Neurologic Surgery
Mayo Foundation and Medical School
Rochester, Minnesota

The use of animals in research, particularly in those aspects of research in which pain is likely to be inflicted, raises numerous complex issues insofar as the investigator's responsibility is concerned (1-4). These issues span areas as diverse as religion, ethics, and social attitudes, as well as the investigator's conscience. Each of these issues varies to some degree from one culture to another.

I believe it is reasonable to assume at the outset that society as a whole accepts the need and justification for carrying out research on animals. It is therefore not necessary to deal here with the moral and theological issue of the investigator's right to take the life of an animal in the pursuit of information which may prove to be of value to the future well-being of human and/or animal life.

The issues that concern us here relate, then, to the manner in which research is conducted, with special reference to the discomfort, suffering, or actual pain to which an animal may be exposed, the overall care provided, and the attention given to the animal's well-being at all times. These issues have been a major concern of many organizations, both national and foreign, involved in research (1, 2). Thus the National Institutes of Health (NIH), the American Physiological Society, and the Canadian Council for Animal Care, among others have issued guidelines governing the use of animals; and the recently constituted International Association for the Study of Pain has appointed a standing committee to study and report on ethical standards for investigation of experimental pain in animals. Furthermore, editorial boards of many scientific journals have policies whereby

evidence of unethical conduct in experimental procedures
results in rejection of manuscripts.

ACQUISITION OF ANIMALS

The responsibilities of the investigator are not limited
to the major issues of discomfort, suffering, and pain, but
include other aspects, such as humane handling and care--a
process that begins with acquisition of the animal. The
guiding principle is that animals should be lawfully
acquired. Thus the legitimate fears of the public regarding
pets will be largely dispelled.

With the exception of small, prolific, rapidly maturing
animals, such as mice and rats, it is generally not feasible
for most institutions to raise animals for research purposes.
Though there are opinions to the contrary, I believe that
State laws which assign unclaimed, impounded animals to
research facilities are a rational, though perhaps incomplete, solution to the problem of acquisition.

CHOICE OF SPECIES

Selection of an appropriate model is an important consideration, particularly at a time when alternative models for
animal research are being emphasized (3). The argument, put
briefly, is: "Why use a lower form of life, such as a frog
or perhaps an invertebrate, rather than a mammal? Even
better, why not do away with animal models altogether and
rely on computer simulation?"

Since it is the investigator's responsibility to make a
choice of models and since, with few exceptions, these will
be animal models, the argument requires careful consideration. rated by carefully designed experimental studies in
animals. What the computer does provide is a superb technique for processing vast amounts of data with great speed
and accuracy and for presenting them in almost any manner th
ments do not necessarily represent the opinions of other
investigators or of any particular group. In some respects,
especially where the issue of research on pain is concerned,
my criteria may be considered far too restrictive by some
investigators. If so, so be it; but my reasons for taking
specific positions on these important issues will be spelled
out in detail and are, of course, open to informed discussion
and rebuttal.

Less advanced animal species have been used for many years in studies of the nervous system. Currently a great deal of basic research is carried out on invertebrate forms, ranging from molluscs to crustacea and insects. The advantages that derive from investigating simple neural networks in these animals, with their large and readily identified neurons, have long been recognized. However, human neural networks are of immense complexity, making extrapolations from lower species to man extremely hazardous.

In this respect one may cite the case of the distinguished experimental psychologist Lashley, who spent a lifetime trying to localize the memory trace in the cerebral cortex of the rat. In one of his last papers, entitled "In Search of the Engram," he stated that he "had learnt a great deal about where memory was not." It certainly did not appear to be localized in any particular part of the cortex, and he concluded that memory is diffusely represented in an equipotent cerebral mantle. However, the situation is not analogous to that in man, in whom the temporal lobe plays a major role in a number of aspects of memory. The attempt to extrapolate from a lower animal to the human resulted in much wasted animal life, effort, and money, and led to a seriously flawed conclusion.

Many other examples could be given of human functions that can be investigated only in higher mammals (motor control, some limited aspects of pain) or for which no animal model exists (speech, symbolic thought).

The choice of an appropriate animal model is thus the responsibility of a fully informed investigator. No one should be a better judge than he or she as to the optimal species for a particular project.

As for computer simulation as an alternative to animal experimentation, since these proposals have been seriously entertained by some, the investigator has the responsibility to decide whether, or to what extent, a computer program can substitute for an animal model.

At the present time and for the foreseeable future it seems clear that the computer will not be a feasible substitute for experiments on animals. The fundamental reason is that a computer cannot acquire data other than those that are generated by carefully designed experimental studies in animals. What the computer does provide is a superb technique for processing vast amounts of data with great speed and accuracy and for presenting them in almost any manner the investigator desires. Much more information can be acquired from an individual experiment in this way, and the greatly improved presentation of data may in some instances assist in formulating hypotheses. In summary, the computer is a valuable tool that can materially increase the yield of

information from experiments, but it is rarely if ever a
substitute for animal models in the investigation of higher
functions.

To suggest that enough data are already available from
previous work, so that from them programs can be generated
and then subjected to a variety of permutations that would
lead to new insights, overlooks an important fact. In any
animal experiment there are numerous variables over which we
have little control, and there are virtually always as many
more about which we as yet know nothing but which may have
very significant influences on the phenomenon under investigation. In real life, which after all is what matters in
biologic research, these variables may be crucial and may
give important clues to entirely unsuspected phenomena that
are sometimes far more important that the original subject of
the study. In a word, computers do not generate new concepts
or acquire new data. They process data and permit the investigator to view it in more manageable or novel ways, and this
may facilitate new hypotheses or insights.

These comments should not be construed as negativism or a
refusal to consider the possibility of alternative models.
Rather they are an attempt at objective assessment of an
issue that has great potential significance for progress in
the biosciences. The validity of the experimental method, as
formulated by Claude Bernard, requires no accolades; the
advances it has engendered in little over a century are the
best testimony to its effectiveness. If alternative models
are to be employed, evidence that they are at least as reliable must be forthcoming before they can be accepted.

There are, of course, alternative ways of studying
selected aspects of animal function--for example, studies of
electrophysiological or pharmacological activity by the use
of isolated organs or tissue slices maintained in controlled
environments. Though the tissue is removed from the animal
and is abnormal in this respect, problems of pain and the
requirement for anesthesia are eliminated.

USE OF MAMMALS IN RESEARCH

For reasons outlined in the previous section, I believe
the case has been made that for many aspects of research
there is no substitute for a higher mammal, that in some
instances a primate may be required, and that in yet others
no nonhuman model exists. The following considerations
regarding principles of handling mammals in research are
probably applicable, with some logical modifications, to
submammalian forms.

The requirements for general maintenance, such as clean, temperature-controlled, well-ventilated housing with day/night artificial-light cycles and acceptable feeding and watering facilities, are dealt with in considerable detail in the Guide for the Care and Use of Laboratory Animals (DHEW Pub. No. (NIH) 78-23) and will therefore not be discussed further. Appropriate veterinary supervision is also indispensable and needs no further emphasis here.

In the following paragraphs I present principles which I believe are acceptable in experimental studies that involve operative procedures of all types. In general, they differ little from the practices followed in surgical care of human patients.

Preoperative Handling of Animals

Considerate handling of animals being prepared for anesthesia is just as important--and perhaps even more so--than with humans, in view of the inability to communicate with an animal that finds itself in a strange, probably frightening environment and surrounded by strangers. There is no excuse for roughness, shouting, or threatening gestures. Such behavior by any of the personnel involved is not only ethically unacceptable, but counterproductive. An excited or frightened animal will require a considerably larger dose of anesthetic to achieve a satisfactory plane of anesthesia than an animal that is anesthetized while quiet and relaxed. In many experimental situations the excess of anesthetic will significantly impair the phenomenon being studied.

General Anesthesia

General anesthesia has the obvious advantage of suppressing not only sensation, but fear as well, and is thus the method of choice. However, in a number of situations, particularly in studies of the central nervous system, a general anesthetic may suppress or so modify a phenomenon that alternative methods of pain control are required. Each of these has shortcomings on either ethical or methodological grounds.

Spinal Animal

Transection of the spinal cord, performed under a volatile anesthetic which is then discontinued, has been extensively used to study the function of spinal and related

structures. From an ethical standpoint it does not appear
objectionable; though consciousness is retained, the animals
do not seem to be adversely affected. The main drawbacks are
technical, including a moderate hypotension, the need for
artificial respiration in cervical-cord transections, and the
isolation of the spinal cord from normal descending modu-
latory influences.

Decerebration

    Transection of the brainstem at an intercollicular level,
performed under a volatile anesthetic which is subsequently
discontinued, is a frequently used method of abolishing
consciousness and sensation. It too is ethically acceptable,
particularly because the deafferented encephalon remains in a
sleeplike state, as determined by the electroencephalogram.
Some technical shortcomings comparable to those of the spinal
animal are, however, present.

Two-Stage Anesthesia

    Because none of the preceding methods is optimal for
certain neurophysiological studies, some investigators have
opted for a two-stage approach: (a) the major operative
procedure is done under a volatile or short-acting anesthetic, which is then discontinued, and (b) a local anesthetic is then injected into the incision edges of the skin
and into areas on which pressure is to be applied by a ster-
eotaxic or similar apparatus, including the internal auditory
canals. It is usually necessary to administer a neuromuscular blocking agent (curare, dexamethonium, or pancuronium)
and to provide artificial respiration by means of an endo-
tracheal catheter.
    The two major ethical problems with this type of proce-
dure are as follows:
    First, the animal is fully conscious, paralyzed, intu-
bated, and dependent on artificial respiration. As I shall
note later, a guiding principle in handling animals is that
the investigator should be willing to experience any procedure within reason to which he will, in the course of an
experiment, subject a conscious animal. Few investigators
would accept this procedure, and none would like it, even
though the investigator has the advantage of knowing what is
happening and that the procedure will be brief and safe.
    Second, administration of a local anesthetic to pressure
points where bars or screws will be used for immobilization--
or to the internal auditory canals, into which ear bars will

be introduced--probably does not adequately control the pain and cannot suppress general pressure. Moreover, the anesthetic effect will wear off after a few hours. In a paralyzed animal there is no way to know whether suffering occurs or when it begins as the anesthesia wears off, and it is only too easy to forget to repeat the anesthetic.

While a theoretical case can be made for the acceptability of this method, personally I cannot endorse it, except when it is performed under the most stringent supervision by an anesthesiologist, when the information to be acquired is of exceptional importance, when the number of experiments is minimal, and when it has been approved by an appropriate committee on animal welfare.

STUDY OF ACUTE PAIN

Study of pain presents one of the major dilemmas for the investigator, not only from an ethical and moral standpoint, but also from the technical aspect (4-7). Two main subdivisions of this problem require consideration: acute pain and chronic pain.

For study of acute pain I believe that the ethical issue is largely resolved when the investigator not only is willing to, but actually has tested the painful stimulus he plans to employ, and <u>will not subject an animal to pain which he cannot readily tolerate himself.</u> This position tends to place definite limits on the degree of suffering which may be inflicted.

Obviously there are situations in which a particularly painful stimulus cannot be tested on a human subject, neither investigator nor volunteer. Whether it is justifiable to test it on an animal is then a difficult ethical issue which should be resolved in conjunction with an animal welfare committee.

A large proportion of research on pain consists in testing the effectiveness of drugs or of certain procedures, such as focal lesions in the nervous system, for the control of pain. A variety of tests--such as the tail-flick, hotplate, shock-avoidance, and shock-titration tests--have been devised for these purposes.

These methods are ethically acceptable because they have a cutoff point determined by the animal.

However, the unavoidable-shock paradigm, which is used to induce stress in an animal, may not, in my opinion, meet humane standards of conduct of research unless the shock delivered is very carefully calibrated to be within the acceptable, though necessarily uncomfortable range.

In other procedures, a drop of dilute formalin is injected subcutaneously, or bradykinin or a similar drug is injected intra-arterially or interperitoneally, or alumina gel is applied to a nociceptive area in the spinal cord or brainstem. In none of these situations is the animal able to control pain in any way. Once again there is an ethical issue which must be settled. The principle that the investigator should test the stimulus on himself should be applied whenever possible.

The acceptability of several of these procedures is highly questionable, in my opinion. But I must emphasize that (a) I speak strictly for myself; (b) these are procedures which I do not do, and therefore I must disqualify myself as an expert witness in this particular area; and (c) decisions as to the acceptability of such procedures must be reached by appropriate committees composed of a reasonably broad spectrum of scientists actively engaged in a variety of these research areas, together with responsible lay persons.

Having said this, I have little hesitation in asserting that almost all investigators who either perform or contemplate undertaking such procedures would rapidly lose enthusiasm for them after having experienced them personally and would probably direct their scientific interests toward other objectives.

I believe it is fair to say that a vast amount can be learned about the problem of acute pain without ever needing to inflict pain that would not be tolerable to most people. Such research is invaluable and can be conducted in an entirely ethical manner. Whether research involving greater pain than this is ever acceptable is an entirely different matter. Personally, I have found no exceptional circumstances under which any such procedures should be done; if they exist, they must be rare indeed.

STUDY OF CHRONIC PAIN

Studies of chronic pain raise even more difficult issues than those posed by studies of acute pain. However, the need for an experimental model with which to study chronic pain is regarded by a substantial number of responsible investigators as pressing (5). This can be readily understood, since most pain problems in the human are of the chronic type, due to arthritis, cancer, back disorders, and so on. Many are intractable and incapacitating, whereas virtually all acute pain can be more or less rapidly and effectively controlled. Furthermore, it seems likely that the mechanisms of chronic pain may differ substantially from those of acute pain.

These are the justifications offered for developing such a model.

However, it is morally and ethically difficult to justify exposing a healthy, pain-free animal to a situation in which it becomes subject to prolonged and constant pain. Those who believe such conduct is acceptable do so on the basis of what they consider to be the greater good--that is, the need to determine the mechanism of such pain in order to devise more effective therapy.

The difficulty with this type of reasoning, quite apart from the ethical issue, is that it is impossible to know much, if anything, about the pain an animal experiences, any more than we can appraise another human being's chronic pain (headache, migraine, cancer pain) other than by his or her description of it. The difficulty--and even the impossibility--of determining whether a patient who complains of chronic pain does in fact have pain, or whether the individual is neurotic or merely malingering, is too well known to require further comment.

Under optimal conditions with humans one can obtain fairly adequate descriptions of the nature of pain in terms of its quality, intensity, distribution, fluctuation, and duration. This, however, requires an intelligent, cooperative, communicative patient. Such information cannot be obtained from animals. Inferences about chronic pain induced in animals would, in my opinion, be nothing more than that and hence of dubious scientific value.

As an example of this dilemma, the phenomenon that has been named autotomy is particularly instructive. When an extremity is made anesthetic in a rat by severing the sensory roots, the animal will frequently begin biting the denervated limb and may end by amputating it. Investigators have inferred from this behavior that the animals were suffering from abnormal sensations and probably from pain, and therefore attacked the affected extremity. However, no one knows that this is so. The animals may behave as they do simply because the limb is clumsy or feels different, and perhaps they become intrigued by the fact that it does not hurt when they bite it. Yet some investigators have felt that this is an appropriate model for studying pain, even though the difficulty in assessing what is actually happening is obvious.

What principles, then, can be suggested to govern the use of animal models to study chronic pain?

First, the model should closely simulate a particular chronic pain syndrome in the human. Otherwise there can be no medical/scientific justification.

Second, the degree of pain should be within a range that a reasonable individual would regard as tolerable. How does one make this determination, however, with no means of communication?

Third, the animal should be able to control the intensity of the pain. The logical objection to this principle is that, given this option, the animal would "turn off" the pain-producing stimulus and keep it off. This objection can be circumvented by recourse to a food reward for keeping the stimulus "on" at a given level, as in experiments with shock-titration techniques.

To sum up: Both the technical and ethical problems related to the development of animal models for chronic pain appear to be formidable. An acceptable model may yet be developed, but it must be subjected to the closest scrutiny to ensure that it is neither valueless, nor ethically unacceptable, nor both.

These considerations leave unanswered the problem of chronic pain in humans. This is an area about which far too little is known and which requires a great deal more attention than it has received. We should not lose sight of the fact that literally millions of human beings live with constant and incapacitating pain--human beings for whom something must be done. Our concern for animal welfare must be balanced against the grief and suffering of these unfortunate victims of painful disease.

What can be done to learn more about the control of pain in these patients? This is not the place to discuss the problem in any depth; suffice it to say that many investigators are now involved in studies on humans suffering from chronic pain. Perhaps this is the situation in which Pope's dictum that "the proper study of mankind is man" should be applied.

IMPLEMENTATION OF HUMANE PRINCIPLES

Guidelines and statements of principles governing research involving animals are already available, as noted earlier. Though varying in detail, they are comparable in substance and, if scrupulously observed, would, I believe, be acceptable to all concerned groups. The issue that is perhaps most troublesome to many is how to implement these humanitarian guidelines, for they are of little avail if they remain nothing more than sterile statements of intent.

Before discussing possible measures to ensure that guidelines are followed, it is important to have some estimate of the magnitude of the problem. The great majority of investigators I have known have been humane and considerate in their contacts with animals, and the vast majority of experiments are carried out under general anesthesia. The problem arises with the occasional investigator who is careless, callous, or inhumane. Though this is an infrequent situation, there is no question that unacceptable procedures have been carried out--and that they will be in the future-- unless appropriate steps are taken to prevent such occurrences.

There is probably no means of assuring beyond all doubt that transgressions will never occur, any more than it is possible to have a crime-free society. It is, however, quite possible to reduce the incidence of infractions of humane procedure to a minimum. I believe that this is best achieved when the director of a research program knows what is going on in the laboratories for which he is administratively responsible, identifies as soon as possible any individual who fails to measure up to acceptable standards, and takes prompt corrective measures.

Experimental protocols are in virtually all instances reviewed by scientific committees at NIH or other sponsoring organizations, which are sensitive to ethical and human-itarian issues.

Finally, the animal research committee in the parent institution exercises a supervisory role over all experi-mental procedures involving animals.

Can anything more be done to ensure adherence to ethical and humane principles? Probably peer pressure is as effec-tive as any other measure, and with heightened awareness in the research community regarding these issues, the likelihood of anyone mistreating an experimental animal has become very significantly reduced.

CONCLUDING REMARKS

There are probably few investigators who do not regret the need to use animals in research, and it is therefore particularly galling when the term vivisectionist is used to describe them. This happens to be an especially reprehen-sible term, since it implies--and to many indicates unequivo-cally--that a fully conscious animal is subjected to surgical and other invasive procedures without anesthesia and hence with the infliction of unbearable pain. This never happens in any reputable research facility, and to impute such an act to an investigator transcends the bounds of fairness and civility. Yet the term vivisection has been employed in the most inflammatory and cavalier fashion for over a century.

The fact is that the technical aspects of operative procedures on experimental animals differ in no way from those carried out daily on humans in thousands of hospitals, yet no one would dream of accusing a surgeon of performing vivisection. The time is long overdue for the self-styled antivivisectionists to reassess their position with regard to this opprobrious term.

In the best of all worlds there would be no disease--no suffering--and hence no need to do research on animals. However, it has not been given to us to live in Utopia. But there is a small and dedicated proportion of the population that, for over a century now, has by its toil delivered humanity from the horrors of rabies, bubonic plague, diphtheria, syphilis, and tuberculosis, to name but a few of the scourges that once decimated whole nations and brought dreadful suffering to millions. Does any rational individual believe that this could have been achieved without the sacrifice of countless rats, mice, guinea pigs, rabbits, cats, dogs, and monkeys?

Devastating epidemics are a thing of the past because investigators made it so. Heart disease, cancer, and degenerative and mental diseases are retreating at an ever-increasing pace, and within a century or less they may have been completely vanquished.

To those who adamantly oppose research using animals I would say: You will stand accountable for a heinous crime, not only against your own race, but against the animals you purport to protect, for they too benefit from parallel advances in veterinary medicine.

It matters not that you have good intentions, for good intentions do not absolve you from awesome responsibility, any more than the good intentions of an incompetent surgeon exonerate him from the burden of the death of a patient.

These comments are not in any way intended as a defense, for investigators do not need to defend themselves or their high calling.

REFERENCES

1. Bowd, A. D., Ethics and animal experimentation, Am. Physiol. 35, 224-225 (1980).
2. Committee for Research and Ethical Issues of the International Association for the Study of Pain, (IASP), Ethical standards for investigations of experimental pain in animals, Pain 9, 141-143 (1980).
3. Hoff, C., Immoral and moral uses of animals, N. Eng. J. Med. 302, 115-118 (1980).
4. Iggo, A., Experimental study of pain in animals--ethical aspects, Adv. Pain Res. Ther. 3, pp. 773-778. Raven Press, New York (1979).

5. Sternbach, R., The need for an animal model for pain, Pain 2, 2-4 (1976).
6. Wall, P. D., Editorial, Pain 1, 1-2 (1975).
7. Wall, P. D., Editorial, Pain 2, 1 (1976).

ANIMAL EXPERIMENTATION AND THE SCIENTIST

Marc E. Weksler

Division of Geriatrics and Gerontology
Department of Medicine
Cornell University Medical College
New York, New York

When I was originally asked to contribute to this forum, I felt that there must have been some mistake, because the welfare of research animals was a subject I knew relatively little about. I was assured, however, that this was exactly the reason for my being invited, and I have come a long way since then in becoming more aware of the issues discussed here. I wish to tell you of my experience as an investigator who has dealt with animals for about 17 years and humans nearly 20 years and about my consciousness with regard to what might best be called experimental subjects, human and nonhuman.

When I was a medical student, we were paid $200 to undergo cardiac catherization, and there was very little concern among us at that time about the problems of the experimental subject. We eagerly took the money, having complete faith that what the professors were doing was ethical, safe, and a contribution to scientific knowledge.

Two years after finishing medical school I was drafted and went to the National Institutes of Health to perform my military service. I went into the laboratory of a world-famous member of the National Academy of Sciences, and he said, "Why don't you go down to the basement and give them a hand with the experimental animals?" I remember opening the door to an animal room and seeing someone with a big asbestos glove holding a rat in one hand and decapitating it with a paper cutter in the other. I experienced the same sinking feeling I had had the first time I entered an operating room and beat a hasty retreat. I said to this investigator, "Maybe I should do some reading to understand what it's all about." The end of the story is that within a week or two I

SCIENTIFIC PERSPECTIVES ON ANIMAL WELFARE

33

was doing the same thing. Clearly I had an emotional reaction, but in actuality the climate was such that one didn't question whether it was appropriate. I discussed my reaction with some of my colleagues serving in the Public Health Service, and they concurred.

My next experience with conscious awareness of these issues was a research opportunity in Great Britain. There, much to my surprise, I had to obtain a license to ensure the humane treatment of animals. You could not study animals unless you were certified. The certification was perfunctory and appeared to have been initiated by a group of animal lovers who imposed their will on the political process. I feel it did not really achieve its purpose and led to less humane treatment of animals.

About 5 years ago I was talking to our Director of Animal Resources at the Cornell Medical School in New York concerning implementation of a rights committee for experimental subjects. I had been involved in the Human Rights Committee during my medical school days and had even then perceived a lack of concern. At Cornell we had instituted a Committee in Human Rights, which was mandated by law, and now it had become necessary to consider the same option for animal subjects.

When we met, we were concerned that an in-house group comprised solely of scientists might be questioned as holding the humane treatment of animals as a secondary interest. Because of this potential criticism, we considered whether outside members of the community, perhaps people active as pet owners and with the humane society, should be placed on this committee. The decision was affirmative, as we felt it was better to select our own committee members than to have them imposed upon us. Our current Animal Welfare Committee, however, does not have outside members, although I think this is worth reconsidering for the future.

The next thing regarding animals that happened in my career was that I became interested in the biology of aging. This could be very frustrating, since the subjects can outlive the investigator. One must investigate not only the lifespan, but also the disease span, the pathologic mechanisms that lead to new diseases among old subjects, and the various conditions that lead to premature death or to the extension of life (1).

The significant ethical issues involved have become clear to me because of some interesting animal experiments. The heart of the issue is whether or not our most important consideration should be the sensations of animals. For example, there are only two ways to extend the maximum lifespan of an animal. One technique is to reduce the body temperature or induce hypothermia. Liu and Walford (2) have shown that if one takes a fish and puts it in water at 15°C rather than 22°C, one can extend its lifespan by up to 50 to 60 percent. The other technique for increasing lifespan is via caloric control. Over 40 years ago McCay et al. (3) showed that undernutrition, as distinct from malnutrition, could dramatically extend the lifespan of rodents. It became apparent, therefore, that some of the most interesting experiments in controlling lifespan in experimental animals would raise questions about the humane aspects of the study and the willing participation of the subjects.

While there did not seem to be an obvious way of starving animals in a humane manner, careful considerations of experimental design permitted such studies to be performed. In a recent investigation (4) the experimental rats were allowed to preselect their own intake. These workers chose a group of animals and carefully measured their food intake. Certain rats ate on the average of 12 grams of chow a day, while others ate 14, 16, 18, or 20 grams. The investigators were able to show, by this far more humane experimental approach, that animals that preselected a lower caloric intake lived significantly longer. In other words, lifespan was inversely proportional to food intake. This experiment is an example whereby creative thinking led the investigators to an experiment that was designed more humanely and led to an even better scientific conclusion.

Several questions come to mind regarding aging research. One is the impossibility of knowing the cause of the animal's death. There are an insufficient number of veterinary pathologists to assist us with diagnosis of diseases in old animals. Thus we are never quite sure whether we are studying a disease that has increased in frequency or severity because of age or the aging process itself. Even more humbling to scientists like myself is the fact that in nearly all papers that report on the physiological, biochemical, and immunological changes that occur as an animal ages, there is a sort of casual statement that a gross autopsy was performed. That means that if nothing abnormal was obvious to our cursory inspection, we described the animal as being normal.

This raises another issue: Should we be concerned about maintaining animals alive through various disease processes, the nature of which is unknown? I feel that diagnosis of disease among elderly animals is far from adequate and that this compromises not only the welfare of the animal, but also--and more importantly--the quality of research on aging. Thus careful thought about humane care of animals should be better for scientific research. Certainly I feel that it is a major shortcoming in the biology of aging.

As a result of my concern and heightened awareness, I have begun reading pertinent articles which I otherwise would

have ignored. I would like to share one of these with you.
A letter reprinted as a feature called "One Hundred Years
Ago," in the British Medical Journal on June 20, 1981 (5)
proves that this is not a new concern. The letter, dated
April 14, 1881, was addressed to Professor Holmgren of
Uppsala from Mr. Charles Darwin in answer to a request for an
expression of his opinion on the question of the right to
make experiments on living animals for scientific purposes.

> Dear Sir-- . . . I have all my life been a strong
> advocate for humanity to animals and have done what I
> could in my writing to enforce this duty. . . . I was
> led to think that it might be advisable to have an
> Act of Parliament on the subject. I then took an
> active part in trying to get a Bill passed, such as
> would have removed all just cause of complaint, and
> at the same time have left physiologists free to
> pursue their researches--a Bill very different from
> the Act which has since been passed [which the
> British people live under to this day]. It is right
> to add that the investigation of the matter by the
> Royal Commission proved that the accusations made
> against our English physiologists were false. From
> all that I have heard, however, I fear that in some
> parts of Europe little regard is paid to the suffer-
> ings of animals, and if this be the case I should be
> glad to hear of legislation against inhumanity in any
> such country. On the other hand, I know that physi-
> ology cannot possibly progress except by means of
> experiments on living animals, and I feel the deepest
> conviction that he who retards the progress of
> physiology commits a crime against mankind. . . . Let
> it be remembered how many lives and what a fearful
> amount of suffering have been saved by the knowledge
> gained of parasitic worms through the experiments of
> Virchow and others on living animals. . . . Dear sir,
> yours faithfully, Charles Darwin.

I have read recently that the number of animals being
used in research in the past decade has dropped dramatically
to about 40 percent of the number used in the previous
decade. New technologies as alternatives to live animal
experimentation have attracted considerable scientific
interest and may be partly responsible for the decline in
animal usage. Cell cloning and test-tube physiology, bio-
chemistry, and immunology have commanded the interest of many
investigators. But I think it would also be naive to ignore
the expense factors at a time of reduced budgets. For
example, when I came to Cornell, we raised antibodies in

rabbits, and when this became economically prohibitive, we started using rats. Today we make large amounts of mono-clonal antibodies by using hybridoma technology and a mouse. I would ask you to consider, therefore, that there has been a considerable restraint in the scientific community with respect to animal research.

At the same time the growing opposition to the use of animals in research is frightening. It seems to me that our society is one which tolerates all persuasions, and those people who hold the views that animals should not be used in research and should not be eaten have the right to express their views. Nevertheless I am frightened by the prospect of legislation which would hamper animal research and so restrict the progress of science. We are clearly not at the point of being able to replace study of the biology of an intact organism with study of intact cells in tissue culture, let alone by punching out data on typewriter keys of comput-ers. However, all of these alternative techniques are used today in aging research.

A group at the Massachusetts Institute of Technology uses computer modeling to study the so-called Hayflick phenomenon, whereby most normal diploid cells, after a period in tissue culture, will no longer grow and will senesce. Hayflick (6) has argued for some time that this represents cellular aging and that it is an important and useful model. Others sug-gest, however, that it is not aging, but differences in the selection of cells that have lost true differentiation as opposed to parental aging. Clearly cellular research receives a great deal of attention in the biology of aging.

One of the important uses of tissue culture assessment of aging is to investigate the function of an organ or a cell free from the aging environment. In my own case, we were never sure whether the immune system, whose function is reduced in aged people or animals, was intrinsically disturb-ed or just compromised because of the elderly environment. It was important therefore to isolate the aging cells of interest and test them free of the elderly environment. One takes the same cells from young and old animals and transfers them to irradiated young animals to see whether the old cells can survive normally in a young environment. Would the old cells retain their impairment out of the old environment, or would they be reconstituted in the young environment? This procedure has been widely used and has no difficulty in receiving Animal Subjects Committee approval. But the use of this in vitro system, which is free of the necessity to sacrifice an animal, has led to very different conclusions from our in vivo work. Current research is aimed at recon-ciling these differences. Clearly, one without the other would have produced a very limited viewpoint, which stresses the importance of having the option to perform both types of experiments in animals.

REFERENCES

1. Committee on Animal Models for Research on Aging, Institute of Laboratory Animal Resources, National Research Council, "Mammalian Models for Research on Aging," 587 pp. National Academy Press, Washington (1981).
2. Liu, R. K., and Walford, R. L., The effect of lowered body temperature on lifespan and immune and non-immune processes, Gerontologia 18, 363-88 (1972).
3. McCay, C. M., Crowell, M. F. and Maynard, L. A., The effect of retarded growth upon the length of lifespan and upon the ultimate body size, J. Nutr. 10, 63-79 (1935).
4. Ross, M.,H., Dietary behavior and longevity, Nut. Rev. 35, 257-65 (1977).
5. No author (reprint of a letter by Charles Darwin), Br. Med. J. 282, 2004 (1981).
6. Hayflick, L., in: "Handbook of the Biology of Aging" (C. E. Finch and L. Hayflick, eds.), pp. 159-188. Van Nostrand Reinhold, New York (1977).

INVESTIGATOR RESPONSIBILITIES
IN ANIMAL EXPERIMENTATION

Perrie M. Adams

Department of Psychiatry and Behavioral Sciences
University of Texas Medical Branch
Galveston, Texas

The requirement of animal experimentation in order to further knowledge is not, as we as responsible scientists recognize, a license to take animal welfare issues lightly or to needlessly inflict harm, pain, or suffering that could be avoided. Abuse of laboratory animals is inconsistent with good and meaningful scientific practice. Nowhere is this more evident than in the behavioral and social sciences, where the measurement of virtually any variable will be influenced by the conditions under which the animal is maintained, handled, and cared for by the investigator.

I believe the scientific community is concerned about the welfare of the laboratory animal, not only as it affects their research, but on ethical grounds as well. Evidence of this concern is demonstrated by the publication and utilization of guidelines for the care and use of animals in research by our scientific societies, as well as by our journals. It is also evident in our peer review process.

It is our responsibility, however, not only to see that our laboratory animals receive the care that is appropriate for them, but also to see that their use in research is not a needless one. This is particularly true as we educate our students. It is our obligation to teach them not only technique, but also what constitutes humane treatment of a laboratory animal. Regardless of the experimental manipulation, humane treatments are available to minimize the suffering and pain involved. It is our obligation as members of the scientific community to assure the public that we are aware of the issues surrounding the welfare of our research subjects, both animal and human, and that we accept our responsibility for protecting our subjects from abuse.

The assumption of this responsibility lies not only with the individual scientist, but with all facets of the scientific community, as this conference so clearly points out.

The attitude frequently expressed by animal welfare proponents is that the scientific community neglects the conditions under which the animal subjects live and the suffering they endure during the research endeavor. I do not feel this view of the scientific community represents the reality of scientific concern, but it does perhaps reflect the poor job we as scientists have done in communicating what we do, why we do it, and how animal welfare fits into our work.

Certainly one of the hoped-for specific outcomes of this conference is an increased awareness by the public of the concern the scientific community has for animal welfare. A second hoped-for outcome is an increased awareness by the scientific community that we must be more explicit about our concerns for animal welfare in teaching our students and reporting our research.

What are some of the possible ways by which we can attempt to increase our fellow scientists' awareness of the welfare of animals used in research? First, we need to have more forums such as this one to allow more discussion of the issues and to demonstrate to those who feel we lack concern for animals that this perception is inaccurate. Second, we can encourage more courses, seminars, and workshops on the ethical issues of doing animal research. Third, we need specific guidelines for teaching our students about the appropriate use of animals in research. Finally, we can recommend that animal care and use committees be used to implement a formal review process of animal research.

Let me comment briefly on each of these areas of consideration.

First, forums such as this conference, the recent conference on the alternatives to animal experimentation, and others provide the broad scientific community and those groups particularly concerned about animal welfare an opportunity to interact and hopefully to improve the communication between them. We as scientists can ill afford to take the posture of an ostrich on this issue.

Second, we should incorporate into our graduate and medical school curriculum courses on the ethical treatment of the research subject, both animal and human. While many medical schools have courses in medical ethics for the practice of medicine, there is a lack of teaching on the ethics of research in general and on the ethics of animal research in particular.

Third, we need to teach our students more than why and how to answer a scientific question. In addition to those questions related to scientific problem-solving, we need to ask:

- Is this a worthwhile experiment? Is it needed, or will the results be a replication of clearly known information?
- Could the scientific problem be better answered in a nonanimal model?
- Is the choice of animal appropriate?
- Is the number of animals to be used appropriate and not excessive?
- Do the procedures employed consider the animals' suffering and attempt to minimize it? In particular, are the procedures for anesthesia, analgesia, postsurgical care, and euthanasia carefully considered relative to the animals' suffering?

While these are only a few of the questions to be considered in designing an animal research study, they serve to raise the students' awareness of these issues. Many other questions should also be asked which pertain to specific research areas or methodologies.

Finally let me comment on the need for animal subject review committees in our scientific community. Those of us who do human research have lived for some time with rules, regulations, Institutional Review Boards (IRB's), and the Food and Drug Administration telling us how to conduct our research. This has forced our approach toward human research to be more conservative and certainly less spontaneous. It would be difficult to ensure--and, I feel, overly restrictive to require--that every scientist who does animal experimentation request approval before conducting each experiment. Rather, it would seem appropriate for the review committee to consider whether the investigator wanting to do research with animals has expertise and experience with the species in question and appropriate physical facilities for housing and caring for the animals. Further, the review committee should conduct at least an annual examination of the facilities and should review with the investigator any incidents involving severe injury or unexpected death to the animals.

Recent media coverage of the use of animals in research has served to make scientists and the public more aware that animal welfare concerns are a part of all responsible scientific endeavors. It is essential that we address issues related to pain and suffering, needless exposure to doses of highly toxic agents, and the excessive use of a particular species when other animal forms or nonanimal alternatives might be adequate to answer the problem.

We, as responsible scientists, must develop the standards and make every effort to ensure implementation of these standards for humane treatment of animals used in research and teaching. Further, we must develop educational programs to ensure that our students learn these standards and develop good judgment in determining the appropriateness of animal utilization in research.

These are goals we should encourage the members of our respective scientific disciplines to support and incorporate into their guidelines for the care and use of animals in research.

SUMMARY OF WORKSHOP ON INVESTIGATOR RESPONSIBILITIES

Harry C. Rowsell

Canadian Council on Animal Care
and
Department of Pathology
University of Ottawa
Ottawa, Ontario, Canada

A. To What Extent Are Scientists Responsibile for Preventing or Minimizing Pain and Suffering?

The ultimate responsibility for preventing animal pain and suffering lies with individual scientists. We should not do anything to an animal that we would not endure ourselves. This is a very difficult issue, however, when it comes to animal models for studies of chronic pain and disease because we cannot define pain in scientific terms. This creates a dilemma, for if scientists do not attempt to define pain, someone or some group less qualified will do it for us. In addition to pain, the animals' fear, anxiety, and deprivation (with frustration and depression in some species) are important considerations. These psychological stresses may more seriously compromise the data we collect and the inferences we draw than does the actual pain itself.

The behavior of experimental animals has generally not been used to its best advantage. Many animals can be trained to accept experimental procedures in a positive manner, thereby avoiding the detrimental effects of forcefully manipulated behavior or forced restraint.

Ultimately the conditions under which experimental animals are handled and maintained depend on the sensitivity and philosophy of the research scientist, who is the effector of any relevant guidelines, rules, or laws. The investigator's degree of concern will determine whether the letter and the intent of the law will be carried out.

Recommendations. Scientists must strive continually to
eliminate unnecessary pain for research animals. Discussions
among scientists regarding currently acceptable practices
should be encouraged. Investigators should spend more time
with their animals to improve their understanding of animal
behavior and to develop a closer relationship with the experimental subject. There is a need to educate investigators
about their responsibilities to the animals they study.

B. How Can We Make Our Colleagues More Aware and Considerate of the Issues?

Scientists tend to lose their sensitivity toward the
animals they study as familiarity and routine set in. The
animal may come to be perceived as just a tool without sense
or feeling. The quality of research then suffers when the
animals are improperly handled or maintained. Investigators
need to be more aware of the needs of experimental animals.
One way to make this point is to collect information on the
effects of improperly handled animals on the outcome of
experiments. Alternatives to the LD_{50} test for toxicity
studies should also be considered. Preliminary studies on
alternative models could be used, followed by a final or
ultimate experiment on the model of choice.

Recommendations. Additional conferences on this subject
should be held. Courses should be given on the ethics of
animal experimentation. Guidelines need to be established
for student teaching. Animal Care and Use Committees could
be more effectively utilized to review facilities and experimental protocols.

C. Do Investigators Have Responsibilities for Reducing Ethical Costs Through the Choice of Optimal Models, Such as Random-Source Dogs Versus Dogs Bred Specifically for Research Purposes?

The issue of using random-source (undefined) dogs versus
the defined animal generated considerable discussion with
some unexpected results. Many participants preferred to use
a defined dog if one was available at a reasonable cost. The
final decision on which source to use should rest with scientist. The general consensus was that research with defined
animals produces more scientifically defensible results, and
some participants felt that defined animals are essential
even for acute, nonsurvival studies. There was considerable
disagreement here, and the issues of economics and of wastage

of life in pounds were raised. The ethical cost doubles when
humane societies are killing 20 million dogs a year and we
raise others to be killed for research. Most felt it was
important that pound-source, undefined dogs be used whenever
a defined dog isn't needed.

The most important use of undefined animals is teaching
and dissection; the second major use is for acute, nonsurvival studies. Pound dogs should be used to train veterinary and medical students. Whether this should be recovery
or nonrecovery surgery was questioned. With respect to
chronic studies, it was generally agreed that the conditioned
random-source dog is the most practical animal to use. If we
do not maximally utilize these animals destined to be killed
in pounds, we are contributing a disservice to society.

Several participants reminded us that because the random-
source dog is truly undefined, we are working with an unknown
gene pool. Pound dogs frequently come from random breeding
of local street stock, and some may, therefore, be more
closely related than we realize. The question remains
whether a randomly selected gene pool is more desirable,
being analogous to the human population we may wish to model.

Recommendation. The scientific community should be
ultimately responsible for solving these questions. The
long-term costs to society of gathering, conditioning, and
establishing the health status of undefined dogs versus
breeding defined animals needs to be considered with respect
to the scientific validity of the data generated, as well as
the economics involved.

D. How Can We Ensure Investigator Responsibility Among Our
Peers?

Training programs are needed for both scientists and
technicians. Additional resources are needed to teach appropriate courses, and these should be required for all individuals involved in animal care and experimentation.

We also need improved interaction of investigators with
their animals, as well as with their support caretakers and
technicians. The contribution of animal technicians is
frequently unrecognized, much less appreciated or rewarded.
Frequently it is the technician who points out inadequacies
to the scientific supervisor or the director of the animal
research facility. Most problems are errors of omission,
rather than acts of deliberate cruelty.

Recommendations. A review system should be set up for
all proposed research which would force investigators to

discuss with other responsible scientists their research
involving animals. On the basis of these discussions, the
protocol should be modified, if necessary, before it is
submitted to the formal Animal Care and Use Committee for
approval. On occasion, a protocol may have to be abandoned
and replaced. Lay and technical representation should be
included in the review process.

All individuals involved in animal care and experimentation should have formal training before being allowed to
pursue such work. The qualifications of personnel should be
subject to review.

E. How Can We Ensure Investigator Responsibility and
    Accountability to the Public?

Is the animal welfare issue the result of misconceptions,
or is it a real problem? It was generally agreed that there
is a problem and that it stems from lack of communication
between scientists and the public.

The public needs to be more aware of why and how research
is conducted on experimental animals. We should have an
open-door policy in laboratories and animal facilities for
the general public, the humane societies, Boy Scouts, Girl
Scouts, other young people, and schools. A closed-door
approach is no longer defensible. Our public image is
tarnished and the press has been attacking scientists with
vigor. Public misconception is a real issue, and so scientists must be encouraged to communicate openly with the
public, rather than being defensive. An open-door policy
costs nothing.

Recommendation. Scientists and institutions need to
participate more in public awareness efforts.

SECTION II

INSTITUTIONAL RESPONSIBILITIES
IN ANIMAL EXPERIMENTATION

RESPONSIBILITIES OF INSTITUTIONS FOR THE WELFARE
OF EXPERIMENTAL ANIMALS

Henry J. Baker
J. Russell Lindsey
Craig A. DaRif

Department of Comparative Medicine
University of Alabama
Birmingham, Alabama

It can be inferred from the objectives of this symposium that assignment of responsibilities for the welfare of experimental animals is not well delineated at present. Who, then, must bear principal responsibility for assuring that animals used in science are treated humanely? Five major categories of organizations operate nationally to influence institutions which sponsor biomedical research and teaching programs utilizing animals. These categories are granting agencies, regulatory agencies, animal welfare advocacy groups, the accreditation association, and the public. We believe that excessive emphasis has been placed on the role of national organizations for resolution of animal welfare issues. It is our premise that individual institutions must be accountable for the welfare of all animals used in their teaching, research, and testing programs.

Why should institutions assume primary responsibility for experimental animal welfare? The vast majority of biomedical teaching and research is conducted in public and private institutions. As a consequence of hosting such programs, institutional leaders usually understand that they are held accountable for compliance with accepted standards of good practice. Biomedical science, including animal experimentation, has reached a level of sophistication and complexity that exceeds the resources of most individual investigators. Therefore, scientists usually are provided with broadly based core resources, such as animal care and use programs, organized and administered by the host institution.

The communal nature of the resource has important beneficial effects on the investigators served. Since the institution sets standards for operation of the resource, the
attitude and performance of individual investigators tend to
be influenced strongly by patterns set by the institution.
Investigators who are not sensitive to animal welfare issues
or who are not skilled in animal research can be persuaded
and motivated best through association with animal welfare
advocates in their own institution. Finally, the host institution alone is able to identify potential problems at the
local level and respond rapidly to protect the welfare of
experimental animals.

What mechanisms can be employed by institutions to assure
that animals are treated humanely and used appropriately in
programs of high scientific quality? How can institutions
demonstrate to external agencies and the public that their
animal care and use programs meet high standards? Since
institutions vary greatly in their mission and organizational
complexity, these questions must be addressed in terms that
are somewhat general.

First and foremost, the administrative officers of the
institution must appreciate the need for an environment of
sensitivity toward humane care and use of experimental
animals. They must be willing to endorse and defend those
who manage the animal resources in their advocacy of experimental animal welfare. Without this high level of understanding and solid backing by the institutional leaders, the
remaining components of the institutional program cannot
function effectively. Direct involvement by a high-ranking
institutional officer in policy matters of the animal
resource program is necessary to translate institutional
commitment into action.

The heart of the commitment by an institution to animal
welfare is the experimental animal resources program. Institutional policies and practices designed to protect the
welfare of experimental animals are implemented through this
program, which must be staffed by professionals and technicians who are knowledgeable, skilled, and sensitive to
animal welfare issues. All participants, from institutional
officers to the investigators, must agree on the institution's operational standards, which should be documented
clearly. It is useful if these standards parallel--or at
least agree in principle with--those accepted by national
agencies that regulate or evaluate animal care and use
programs.

Effective implementation of institutional objectives is
highly dependent upon support for the animal resource program
by the investigator community. Institutional objectives on
animal welfare issues are occasionally served best by

policies and procedures that may not be readily accepted by some investigators. In such instances the investigators must understand the value of the communal organization and support the common goal. In return, investigators are accorded the substantial benefits of affiliation with an animal resources program recognized as meeting high standards.

In this type of institution/investigator relationship, it is implied that institutional leaders understand and approve of the animal experimentation activities of all investigators. Indeed, the institution's ability or willingness to defend a given project against potential public criticism is a useful test of the advisability of the project itself. Confidence that this test can be met must come from thorough review of each project at the proposal stage, as well as monitoring of the actual conduct of the experimental protocol. Presubmission review of research proposals presents serious logistical problems, which are compounded if the process is highly formalized or extensive. The principal purpose of review at this stage is to assure that investigators propose experimental animal procedures that are humane and scientifically sound. If procedures are proposed which are inherently painful, use of pain-relieving drugs must be indicated, or clear justification must be offered for not using such drugs. The applicant also should indicate in the proposal the status of the sponsoring institution regarding compliance with applicable laws, policies, and accreditation.

Direct interaction between the applicant and the specialist in laboratory animal medicine at the institution is an effective means of presubmission review. It is imperative that applicants address animal welfare issues thoroughly in their proposals. Hopefully, granting agencies will fulfill their obligation in the review process by assuring that all applications proposing to use experimental animals are reviewed by experts in animal research charged with responsibilities that include animal welfare. Since some research projects and most teaching programs that use animals are funded internally, it is important that a mechanism be established to assure equivalent preview of these proposals.

Review of ongoing research is actually more important than preview of proposed procedures, but it rarely is accorded appropriate attention. Modification of a research proposal occurs frequently, and occasionally the revised protocol differs significantly from the original submission in details of experimental animal procedures. Furthermore, direct observation of a procedure is often more revealing than a brief written description. Therefore, a mechanism should be provided by the institution for periodic review of all active projects using animals. One mechanism to accomplish this goal is registration of researchers using

animals, with the institutional officer given responsibility
for animal research affairs. Registrants would be visited
and interviewed at intervals by designated institutional
professional staff. Depending upon their findings, additional attention by a committee of peers might be required. Such
a formal internal review process would provide the best
possible safeguard against animal abuse and would greatly
strengthen the position of the institution against unwarranted criticism.

The skill, understanding, and attention of scientists to
details of animal experimentation vary widely and are frequently inadequate. The reasons for this weakness include
dependence on outdated concepts, pressures of other responsibilities, lack of sensitivity to humane issues, failure to
recognize the contributions of laboratory animal specialists,
mistaken appraisal of their own ability in animal experimentation, and excessive reliance on technicians with
inadequate training in methods of animal experimentation. No
competent scientist would ask students or technicians to
perform a chemical analysis without substantial evidence that
they were technically competent to perform such laboratory
techniques. However, it is not uncommon for scientists to
assign animal research procedures of equivalent complexity to
individuals with no formal technical training or experience.
It is easily within the capacity of institutions to require
appropriate training of those performing animal experimentation and to provide academic and technical training opportunities. This approach would provide immediate benefit to
experimental animals and would likely persuade technicians
and scientists in training that animal welfare and competent
animal research are inseparable from good science.

Complex institutions have long recognized the value of
external review to assist in self-assessment and to enhance
public confidence. Few institutional programs benefit more
from comprehensive external evaluation than animal resource
programs. Fortunately, in the United States an organization
exists which facilitates this process. The American
Association for Accreditation of Laboratory Animal Care
(AAALAC) has conducted thorough reviews of animal resource
programs since 1965. Currently more than 457 institutions
conducting animal research in this country utilize AAALAC's
review process to demonstrate compliance with national standards of experimental animal care and use. Accreditation
review does not involve some scientific aspects of animal
experimentation and therefore does not substitute for independent assessment by granting agencies. However, accreditation does provide valuable evidence to such agencies that
those components of an institution's program specifically

addressed in the Guide for the Care and Use of Laboratory Animals are of high quality. Institutions must provide assurance to the public that their policies and programs are functioning to protect the welfare of experimental animals. Mechanisms to accomplish this are not well defined or simple. Large institutions should start this effort with their own students, staff, and faculty. Internal publications that feature institutional programs can serve as a useful vehicle for this purpose. Seminars and lectures dealing with animal experimentation and experimental animal welfare are good opportunities to educate the institutional community in the elements of a sound program. Involvement of students and technicians in institutional committees concerned with animal experimentation strengthens the credibility of these programs.

Community leaders of animal welfare groups who accept the benefit of animal research should be given opportunities to interact with institutional advocates of animal welfare. Presentations given by institutional representatives to animal welfare groups provide an opportunity for broader interaction with those having the greatest concern about these issues. If done well, a presentation which describes a strong institutional program can effectively reduce most individuals' concern about the welfare of laboratory animals used at the institution.

In summary, individual institutions have a clear obligation to protect the welfare of animals used in the teaching, research, and testing programs that they sponsor. Their opportunities to evaluate the status of animal welfare and to influence individuals immediately involved in animal research programs are far greater than those of any other organization. In the final analysis, the best hope for humane use of experimental animals rests in the hands of sensitive, honorable people within the institution who are given the responsibility and authority to protect animal welfare in the laboratory.

SWEDISH LAW ON LABORATORY ANIMALS

Karl Johan Öbrink

Department of Physiology
Uppsala University
Sweden

The Swedish Animal Welfare Act of 1944 states that experiments on animals are not permitted, but some exceptions are made. University laboratories, for example, are allowed to use animals in experiments, but the experiment must be supervised by an authorized manager. If suffering is expected during the course of the experiment, the animal must be given anesthesia or other pain-relieving treatment whenever possible. The law is enforced by the Swedish Board of Agriculture and administered by local health authorities.

In 1979, the Swedish Parliament passed amendments to the law. Three new provisions were made:

- A program of "destination breeding"--special breeding of animals to be used exclusively for experimental purposes.
- Board of Agriculture approval of all facilities housing laboratory animals.
- Establishment of ethical committees to advise the research worker at the planning stage of an animal experiment.

I will discuss this latter provision because it appears to be unique to Sweden and could serve as a model for other countries.

The ethical committees consist of equal numbers of scientists, animal or laboratory technicians, and laymen. Their role is purely advisory. They act as an extended conscience of the scientist to help him or her determine whether the intended experiment is justified in relation to the expected experimental value.

The new regulations resulted from an initiative by Swedish scientists, members of the Scandinavian Federation of Laboratory Animal Science (Scand-LAS), and the Swedish

Medical Research Council.   Their   concern   was   the   ethical
problems that arise whenever a new experiment is started.   A
judgment must be made to weigh the severity of the experiment
for the animals with the goal of the experiment.   Normally
the scientist makes this judgment.   But often scientists
think in terms of the end result of the experiment and may
fail to see the risks involved to the experimental animal.
Those risks might be avoided if the proposed project is first
reviewed by somebody else, a fellow-creature.   And so, the
idea of ethical committees was born.

The ethical committees were pilot tested in Uppsala--one
of Sweden's six university regions--for a period of 3 years.
Uppsala has two universities (Uppsala University and the
Swedish University for Agricultural Sciences), several
research institutes, and a pharmaceutical industry.   All
participated in the pilot experiment.   The general experience
with the ethical discussions was good.   Research workers
especially felt that they benefited from the advice of the
committees and noted these advantages:

- A shared responsibility for ethical judgment.
- Improved communication between research laboratories and
  the general public.   This has reduced the suspicion of
  cruelty going on "behind locked doors" in the
  laboratories.
- Development of mutual understanding of the need for animal
  experiments in medical and biological research as well as
  for the promotion of animal welfare and ethical
  consciousness.

To make the work of the ethical committees reasonably
uniform, the Board of Agriculture has classified experiments
according to the degree of discomfort for the animal (see
table 1).

Those experiments with practically no interference with
or suffering for the animals (Categories 1 and 2) are
excluded from review altogether.   All other experiments where
animal suffering is anticipated.

A group of three--one scientist, one technician, and one
lay person--is selected to discuss the project with the
scientist.   Based on the research worker's description of the
planned experiment, this small group decides whether the
project is acceptable, whether it may be modified to make it
less painful for the animal, or whether it can be performed
with nonanimal systems.   When the research worker and the
group have agreed upon the procedure, the experiment may be
started.

The full committee consists of a large number of members
so as to cover all laboratories using animals.   They are

TABLE 1

SWEDISH CLASSIFICATION OF RESEARCH EXPERIMENTS

Procedure	Example
1. Experiments which, with or without operation, are expected to cause only negligible pain or agony.	Injections, blood sampling, tube feeding, behavioral experiment without significant restraining of the animal, anesthesia to make the animal manageable.
2. Experiments carried out on anesthetized animals, which do not wake up again.	Blood pressure measurement, removal of organs for histological or biochemical investigation or experiments on surviving organs or parts of organs.
3. Experiments with painful stimulation of unanesthetized animals, which cause the animal short-lasting, light pain.	Behaviorial experiments with flight or avoidance reactions.
Operations are carried out under anesthesia or some other painkiller, but the animal will wake up again or experience the cessation of the action of the painkiller. The animal can then have transient post-operative nausea, more or less severe.	From biopsies, exposure of blood vessels, implantation of chronic catheters, gonadectomy by standard methods, simple central nervous system lesions to extensive surgical operations, burns.
4. Experiments on unanesthetized animals of whom some can be expected to become seriously ill or be caused significant pain or significant agony.	Toxicity testing, production of radiation sickness, certain infections, stress and shock experiments, production of pain clearly above the threshold level, behavioral experiments with significant restraining of the animal, e.g., fixation.
5. Experiments on unanesthetized and curarised (or equivalent) animals.	Certain physiological and pharmacological experiments on the nervous system.

notified of the decision of the small subgroup. Private
industry laboratories are included in this review procedure.
In cases of experiments that must be kept secret--when
patents are involved, for example--the descriptions of the
experiments are not publicized. Otherwise all the decisions
are reported to the local health authorities.

A Central Committee for Laboratory Animals in Sweden
coordinates the actions of the Ethical Committees. It also
distributes funds that are placed at its disposal by the
Swedish Parliament for development of alternative methods to
animal experiments.

INSTITUTIONAL RESPONSIBILITIES:
THE COMMITTEE'S ROLE

James G. Fox

Division of Comparative Medicine
Massachusetts Institute of Technology
Cambridge, Massachusetts

As Franklin Loew has eloquently stated in his paper on "Developments in the History of the Use of Animals in Medical Research" in this conference, the use of animals in biomedical research is etched in antiquity. However, concern for the responsibilities of institutions that foster and nurture animal experimentation is a much newer concept with far-reaching implications, including legal, moral, and fiscal considerations.

Not until late in the 19th century did the British Cruelty to Animals Act of 1876 establish the first national law regulating the use of animals in scientific endeavors. This law, which is still in effect, clearly focuses the responsibility for animal experiments on the investigator, and the responsibility is implemented in the form of a licensure program. The basic license allows the individual to perform animal experiments ,only on anesthetized animals; various additional certificates are needed for the scientist to conduct other experiments. In addition, the application must have a form of peer review, i.e., it must be signed by the president of a learned society and a university professor in a branch of medical science. The institutional responsibility consists of conformance to the stated principles of the law and acceptance of inspection on a regular basis (1).

The British system of laboratory animal care and use regulation was recently reviewed and contrasted with the U.S. and Canadian systems (2). The author concluded that British scientists are more aware of their law and regulations than are their counterparts in Canada or the United States. However, the physical state of animal facilities and animal care technology in the United States and, to a certain extent, in Canada exceeds that of the United Kingdom. In the United States, followed by Canada, veterinarians are far more numerous, experienced, and trained in the specialty of laboratory animal medicine than in Britain. He considers this a logical outome of the U.S. law, the Animal Welfare Act, which places institutions employing scientists, rather than the scientists themselves (as in the United Kingdom), in the legally responsible position. The Canadian system and situation tend to occupy a middle ground between those of the United States and the United Kingdom (1,2).

If this analysis is correct, does it imply that the most effective means of providing humane care is to place broader and more comprehensive responsibilities on the institutions? One method of coping with increased accountability on the part of the institution—and at the same time incorporating investigator responsibility and peer review—is the use of a committee framework. The (Laboratory) Animal Welfare Act (Public Law 89-544), enacted in 1966, partially accommodates this philosophy. It stipulates that the attending veterinarian—or an institutional committee of at least three members, one of whom must be a veterinarian—certify that the type and amount of anesthetic, analgesic, or tranquilizing drug administered to an animal during an experimental procedure were appropriate. California Institute of Technology neurobiologist John M. Allman, who uses nonhuman primates to study brain organization, was reported to use this law to justify his views:

> People don't realize that we are already extensively reviewed. In my work I must follow the ethical codes laid down by the National Institutes of Health and the American Physiological Society, among others. And we might have a surprise visit at any time from the U.S. Department of Agriculture's [USDA] inspectors. It's the USDA field veterinarians who do the enforcing. Believe me, these inspections are anything but routine, and these fellows have a great deal of power. Because their reports can adversely affect federal funding, their recommendations are, in reality, orders.
> More than that, we are all required to keep detailed reports on all our animal experiments. And if pain or surgery is involved, we must tell them what anesthetics we used and in what dosages, what postoperative pain relievers and care were given, and so on. These reports are filed annually with the USDA, and they keep tabs on what goes on all over the country.(3)

Unfortunately, these comments fail to acknowledge that (because of exemptions) millions of rats and mice used annually do not fall under the review of the USDA system, nor does current USDA law require review of all aspects of animal experimentation being conducted at the institution.

In an attempt to respond to the numerous pressures being exerted on Congress related to the use of animals in biomedical experimentation, the Subcommittee on Science, Research, and Technology in the House of Representatives recently proposed legislation that would shore up the institution's Animal Care and Use Committee's responsibilities. Under the proposed legislation a research entity, i.e., the institution, in order to be eligible to receive a Federal award for the conduct of research, experimentation, or testing involving the use of animals, must provide the Federal agency with a Statement of Assurance. The bill specifies:

> In order to qualify for a Federal award, a research entity must have established an institutional animal care committee of at least three members; at least one member is a veterinarian; at least one member is not affiliated with the research entity or parent organization and is responsible for representing the concerns of the surrounding local community regarding the welfare of animal subjects; and not more than three members are from the same administrative unit of the research entity.

Among the Animal Care and Use Committee's responsibilities would be review of research protocols in progress involving the direct use of conscious animals, evaluation of these protocols for compliance with the experimental design of the original approved proposal, and filing of inspection reports with the responsible Federal agency evaluating compliance. Each member of the committee would be responsible for notifying the USDA (in writing), as well as the responsible Federal funding agency and any applicable accrediting agency, of any seriously deficient animal care conditions which require attention and which have been persistently neglected, despite notification to the research entity.

Furthermore, the bill stipulates that a research entity cannot receive a Federal award, after the enactment of this act, unless--in any research involving the direct use of conscious animals or chronic, long-term invasive surgical procedures--a veterinarian has been employed in the planning of such procedures; appropriate assurances have been given for the use of tranquilizers, analgesics, or anesthetics, including a full description of the substances, amount, and frequency of use in any case involving surgery or other invasive procedures; and a justification has been provided for anticipated animal suffering in terms of demonstrable benefits of the research (4).

The intent of the legislation appears to be to ensure the presence of a noninstitutional representative on the committee; to provide peer review; to evaluate the expected contribution of the research versus the discomfort of animals subjected to experimental manipulation; and finally, not to rely solely on the USDA Animal Welfare Act and its inspection services, but to go beyond their current impact on animal welfare issues.

If this legislation is enacted, it obviously would place the institutional committee in a position of weighty responsibility and would certainly tax the personnel and economic resources of the parent institution. As an analogy, the existing Human Use Committee mandated by Federal agencies in 1978 requires a similar research protocol review. Experience to date indicates that this process entails considerable involvement of the faculty and economic resources of the institution.

To alleviate the logistical and other problems inherent in committee review, the review of ongoing and proposed research could be placed under the purview of the institution's animal resources program, where initial interaction and protocol review between the investigator and the laboratory animal medicine specialist could take place. Full committee review would be required on a selected basis.
Dr. Baker has stated earlier in this conference that the formalized review process, with latitude to tailor the review process to meet individual institutions' needs, provides the best possible safeguard against inhumane animal experimentation and possible unwarranted criticism against the institution.

REFERENCES

1. McPherson, C. W., in "Laboratory Animal Medicine," (James G. Fox, Bennett J. Cohen, and Franklin M. Loew, eds.). Academic Press, New York (in preparation).
2. Loew, F. M., in "British, Canadian and U.S. Patterns in Regulating the Use of Animals in Research: A Report to the Animal Welfare Foundation of Canada," pp. 1-16. Animal Welfare Foundation of Canada, Thornhill, Ontario (1981).
3. Rosenfeld, A., Animal rights vs. human health, Science 2, 19-21 (1981).
4. Association for Biomedical Research. Regulatory Alert 4, April 29 (1982).

SUMMARY OF WORKSHOP
ON INSTITUTIONAL RESPONSIBILITIES

Richard C. Simmonds

Department of Laboratory Animal Medicine
Uniformed Services University of the Health Sciences
Bethesda, Maryland

A. What Is the Institution's Role and Responsibility
Relative to Research with Experimental Animals?

Institutional responsibilities go beyond academia and
pertain also to industry, as well as Federal, State, and
local government laboratories. Institutions have the ultimate and legal responsibility for the actions of scientists
using animals in research. In fact, however, this responsibility is a continuum from the animal care staff through the
investigator to the institution's top administrator. The
principal investigator of a research project is the effector
and has the primary responsibility for assuring humane and
appropriate treatment of experimental animals. His/her
responsibility cannot or should not be delegated.

The institution has the responsibility not only to review
the animal-subjects protocols for new grants, but also to
continuously monitor ongoing research. Experimental design
can change during the course of a project. Should the Animal
Care and Use Committee be responsible for assurance that only
approved procedures and protocols are being carried out?

In the event of an alleged animal abuse, both the principal investigator and the institution should be culpable.

An internal institutional Animal Care and Use Committee
can be an effective mechanism for achieving the institution's
full responsibility relative to animal issues, provided that
four conditions are met:

1. The composition of the committee should include
"disinterested" persons, such as technical staff, students,
and graduate students, and might include members of the lay

public. (The latter suggestion did not meet with unanimous approval.)

2. To be effective, the committee must report directly to the highest administrative officer of the institution, such as the President or Vice-President for Research.

3. The institution's Supervisor of Animal Care or Director of Animal Facility should be a member of the committee but not the chairman. There was unanimous agreement on this point to assure credibility with both peers and the public.

4. The committee should review all research protocols. Most participants agreed with this proposal, although some had reservations because the sheer volume of protocols in some large institutions (up to 4,000 annually) precludes such review.

One way to handle this number of proposals is to adopt a review process like that used in Sweden, where a pool of reviewers is established that is large relative to the number of protocols to be reviewed (see Professor Öbrink's paper). The review committee is made up of about one-third scientists, one-third lay people, and one-third technicians and others who work in science. An investigator who wishes to begin a project seeks out a local scientist committee member and discusses the protocol on a one-to-one basis. If there are no major problems, the protocol is submitted to the scientists' group, which selects one member from its own and each of the other two groups. A face-to-face discussion is then arranged with all three committee representatives and the investigator. Any identified concerns are worked out, so that the protocols are eventually approved. The system has worked well to date. The key here is to have a large pool of reviewers.

Licensure of individual investigators, as occurs in England, was unanimously considered to be ineffective and would almost certainly create an unmanageable bureaucracy for a country as large as the United States.

The importance of strong administrative support for the animal care program was emphasized. If the administration is not truly behind the program, investigators will be less motivated to pay attention to such matters. This brought up the difference between a Federal regulation or law, such as the Animal Welfare Act, and a set of guidelines like the National Institutes of Health (NIH) Guide for the Care and Use of Laboratory Animals. The previous issue of the Guide became a regulation (Federal Register, April 23, 1974).

It was universally agreed that the current NIH Assurance Program for protection of research animals was ineffective. In contrast, the U.S. Department of Agriculture's (USDA) inspection system can be reliable and is working effectively in some locations. The effectiveness of this mechanism for improving and monitoring animal care is totally dependent on the competence and experience of the local inspector. The USDA is continually working to improve its system and welcomes suggestions (budget cuts notwithstanding).

Voluntary outside inspection and review systems, such as that of the American Association for Accreditation of Laboratory Animal Care (AAALAC), were considered to be very effective and to contribute to better care and experimentation. In some views the AAALAC system should become law, although it was recognized that considerable Federal funds would be needed to enable institutions to comply on a nationwide scale. It was agreed that this would be a worthwhile goal to achieve.

It was also generally agreed that current animal welfare laws and animal care and use guidelines would be adequate to assure humane and proper care and use if more effective mechanisms for their application were implemented.

Recommendations. NIH should include a person knowledgeable in animal care and use issues as a member of each site-visit team and should withhold funds from any program which does not include appropriate animal care provisions (i.e., does not comply with the Guide).

USDA should increase the priority given to enforcement activities for the animal welfare laws and should develop and implement procedures to assure the competence of its inspectors (e.g., closer field supervision by regional directors and better training of veterinary medical officers).

All institutions using animals in research and teaching programs must develop procedures for assuring that persons involved in the care and use of animals are knowledgeable about--and sensitive to--the legal, scientific, and ethical issues. This implies that training is needed for everyone, from the most senior professional to the junior support staff. It should be mandatory, much like radiation safety training.

Mechanisms must be developed to increase the availability of new information about appropriate and specific animal models for specific areas of interest. Better models and improved animal care and use make for better science.

SECTION III

FUNDING AGENCY RESPONSIBILITIES
IN ANIMAL EXPERIMENTATION

RESPONSIBILITIES OF FUNDING AGENCIES
FOR ANIMAL EXPERIMENTATION

Carlos E. Eyzaguirre

Department of Physiology
University of Utah School of Medicine
Salt Lake City, Utah

The purpose of this paper is to present the granting
agencies' role and responsibilities in animal experimentation. First of all, I should make clear that I do not
officially represent any government or private organization.
I am only a scientist and experimenter in biomedical research
who has been doing this kind of work for over 30 years.
Perhaps the only reason that I can address this problem with
a minimum of authority is that I have served on several
National Institutes of Health (NIH) study sections over the
last several years. Therefore, my comments do not represent
any official view but only those of a concerned individual
who has had some experience in the process of granting funds
to various investigators and institutions.

HISTORICAL BACKGROUND

Perhaps it would not be out of place to start with a
short historical background, which may help us reach some
conclusions for the present and the future. As indicated
elsewhere in this conference, mass use of animals for
experimental purposes dates from early Christian times. Its
nature and frequency have varied with the philosophical and
political atmosphere in which scholars have practiced animal
experimentation. Three major tendencies have developed over
the years with regard to animal research: (a) its use as a
method in biologic and medical research; (b) its institutionalization in the latter part of the 19th century; and (c)

the emergence of opposition to animal experimentation, the modern antivivisection movement. I will deal only with the historical aspects of institutionalization of animal experimentation.

Claude Bernard's classic <u>Introduction to the Study of Experimental Medicine</u>, published in the 1860's, presents the philosophical rationale for the new physiology, which, incidentally, is my field. During the same period the spread of research in the German university system affected the medical sciences, just as it affected all of the natural sciences. New university positions required aspirants to establish their competence by virtue of successful experimental research. Therefore, the situation we have today is not new. Research laboratories pursued animal experimentation by using surgical ablations, pharmaceutical substances, or infectious agents.

Since the 17th century it had been proclaimed that great benefits to the clinical practice of medicine would come from the experimental approach. However, it was not until the last decade of the 19th century that support among the bulk of the medical profession and the university authorities led to making resources available for experimental medicine. At that time the medical professions of northern Europe and North America took up the standard of experimental medicine, not only because of its value, but as a test for professional competence to exclude the unorthodox and the older, more traditional members of the profession.

Spectacular medical advances attracted public attention and acclaim. The emergence of immunology in the 1880's was probably the most important single accomplishment that convincingly demonstrated the intellectual validity of the experimental approach and its practical benefit. Obviously, all the discoveries were based on experiments on living animals and eventually affected the lives of millions of people. Thus, vivisection and animal experimentation received the enthusiastic support of the medical establishment and governments. Advancements in chemotherapy, surgery, and preventive medicine, among many others, stimulated a commitment to experimental medicine in virtually every developed nation by the third decade of the 20th century. Again, what we are seeing today is an extension of what happened many years ago.

INSTITUTIONAL INVOLVEMENT IN THE CARE AND USE OF ANIMALS FOR EXPERIMENTATION

At the present time we have a highly organized system for execution of research. In the biomedical area it is obvious that the main provider of funds and guidelines is the U.S. Government through such agencies as the NIH. The guidelines and instructions to institutions and investigators deal in detail with the welfare of animals used for experimentation. Nevertheless, the ultimate responsibility for animal welfare rests with the individual investigator, no matter how good the guidelines and the institutional care. If investigators are not careful or are inhumane in the treatment of animals, the ultimate result will be suffering and mistreatment.

We have to face realities. It is impossible to police every laboratory in the country for 24 hours every day to ensure that proper treatment is given to these animals. At least in the field of physiology, which I know fairly well, many experiments end after midnight, when there is not a soul in the building except for the investigators dealing with the particular research. Humane use of the animal is then entirely in the hands of the investigators. The bottom line is that we are dealing with a moral problem, and the ultimate result will be determined by the moral principles of the investigators themselves.

Laws governing experiments on animals vary in different countries. But no law forbids painful experiments or requires that the experiment be of sufficient importance to outweigh the pain inflicted. The first law specifically regulating experiments was the British Cruelty to Animals Act of 1876. This law, which has not been amended, requires the use of an anesthetic except when insensibility frustrates the object of the experiments. But the law does not deal with the question of whether or not the experiment is worth the pain inflicted. In toxicity tests of cosmetics, anesthetics are not used because of the possibility that they might distort the result of the test. Therefore, such experiments are permitted in Britain as well as in several other countries.

In the United States, the Animal Welfare Act of 1970 determines standards for housing, transportation, and handling of animals. However, the Act does not control the nature of the experiment, except for requiring a statement that when painful experiments are performed without anesthesia, this is necessary to achieve the research objective. Furthermore, the law specifically disavows any intention of interfering with the design or performance of the researchers' experimentation. Moreover, institutions not

receiving Federal funds and not involved in interstate
commerce do not have to comply.

A 1972 West German law requires the use of alternatives
to experiments on animals whenever possible. Similar amendments have been proposed in Britain, Denmark, and Holland,
but it remains to be determined what constitutes an acceptable alternative. Many countries, including France, Spain,
Brazil, and Japan, have no legislation regulating experiments
on animals.

FUNDING AGENCIES RESPONSIBILITIES

It seems to me that the first step in ensuring animal
welfare must be taken at the Study Section level. When grant
proposals are reviewed, it is essential for the Study Section
members to make sure that the number of animals to be used is
not excessive and beyond the needs of the experimentation to
be performed. For instance, it is not uncommon to review
proposals which request practically one animal per day for
studies which really do not need more than one animal per
week. Since the budget is the message, it is easy for Study
Section members to reduce that particular budget with an
admonition that the number of requested animals is excessive.
This may help to improve the disquieting picture of unnecessary animals used in experimentation.

The great majority of animals used for experimentation
are used by drug firms, sometimes to test agents not related
to biomedical research, such as cosmetics. For instance, the
use of the LD_{50} test (lethal dose 50 percent) has been widespread for many years, and each test requires the sacrifice
of up to 100 animals. At times this can be absurdly wasteful, as when used to study nontoxic substances. Nevertheless, the LD_{50} test has become standard in testing the
toxicity of all substances.

Some biologic agents can now be tested in vitro or by a
modified assay in which test animals reach a well-defined
point of sickness, rather than death. For instance, in
evaluating the potency of an antitetanus vaccine, one can
check for paralysis of the mouse's hind limbs. One does not
have to kill the mouse to know that the antitoxin is too
weak. The World Health Organization (WHO) has suggested the
use of cell cultures as an alternative to the LD_{50} test. WHO
accepts either method, requiring only that a laboratory
wishing to adopt the cell culture procedure calibrate it with
the LD_{50} test.

In some ways the Federal Government has been responsible for perpetuating the LD_{50} test. The Environmental Protection Agency and the Food and Drug Administration require every new chemical to be tested by the LD_{50}. If a company wishes to manufacture and transport a chemical, it must be tested by the LD_{50}. Otherwise the law requires that it be handled as an extreme poison. Therefore, a granting agency does have a responsibility and can do something about wasteful use of animals. As indicated before, the budget is the message, and some guidelines in this respect should be available to all investigators receiving government support.

HUMANE TREATMENT

There are indeed guidelines from NIH about decent treatment of animals. But as indicated above, the ultimate responsibility rests with the investigator. Certainly Study Sections can do and have done some policing in this respect. Usually Study Section members are careful in evaluating whether a given test or research will provoke undue suffering to the animal. However, there are gray areas where sometimes the experiment will necessarily cause some suffering to the animal. This is clearly the case when analgesic drugs or opiates are tested. The usual procedure is to run a series of tests, inflicting various degrees of pain to various animals, then delivering the drug and attempting to determine from each animal's physical manifestations when its pain has subsided.

I do not know offhand how to avoid this problem because obviously pain-killing substances cannot be properly tested in anesthetized animals. At the same time, it is clearly cruel to test such drugs in nonanesthetized animals. Perhaps a conference about this subject should be convened with the participation of a good number of experts in the field of pain. It may be possible to develop methods which will not produce undue discomfort to the animals and will still get the desired result. Obviously this is something for the experts to decide. Nevertheless, one should not avoid the issue, and serious steps should be made in the direction of eliminating suffering to animals whenever possible. Granting agencies are in a unique position to do something about this.

ACUTE VERSUS CHRONIC EXPERIMENTS

To a neurophysiologist like myself, acute experiments in general do not present a moral dilemma. In fact, in most cases animals are anesthetized, and therefore pain is absent. The investigator records nerve discharges from various parts of the nervous system using electrophysiologic techniques. Animals such as cats can survive very well during long hours of experimentation, and all the procedures are done painlessly, even when otherwise painful or convulsant drugs are used. At the end of the experiment the animal is sacrificed with a lethal dose of an anesthetic, such as pentobarbital sodium, without ever recovering consciousness.

A problem may arise when one is doing chronic experiments, where various portions of the nervous system may be altered by implanting drugs or by surgically ablating some areas. Naturally these animals are going to be in a very abnormal state; otherwise the experiment would be useless. Here again the granting agencies can do something about the welfare of the animals. First of all the Study Sections, initially responsible for the funding of such an application, should clearly determine whether those experiments are necessary. If they are, the Study Sections can indicate clearly and in no uncertain terms that the care of these animals should be comparable (within some limits) to the care of a human being in a similar situation. The Study Section should convey this to the Council of the appropriate Institute, which is ultimately responsible for the funding of the grant. The Council in turn should transmit this proviso to the institution and the investigator who will receive the funds. This requirement should not incur additional expense to reputable institutions, since most of them have well-staffed vivaria with proper facilities for the care of "chronic" animals. If an institution does not have the personnel or the facilities for this purpose, it should not be granted the award.

One could legitimately ask what is to be gained by this approach, when present policies already address such concerns? Well, I believe a little nudge here and there from the granting agency has a salutary effect. Most people follow the Golden Rule: "He who has the gold makes the rules." And most State and private schools or institutions are usually very keen on complying with government regulations for obvious reasons.

SPECIES INVOLVED

Historically, there has been a tendency to be more humane to cats and dogs, while large farm animals, such as horses and cows, and smaller animals, like rats and mice, have been accorded less than equal consideration--not to mention cold-blooded species, like frogs, turtles, and invertebrates. As far as I am concerned, all these species should receive equal treatment. Morally, one cannot be humane to cats and dogs and be less so to rats and mice or to farm animals. Any visit to a slaughterhouse will confirm my point.

The use of the Draize test is pertinent here. According to Federal law, each new cosmetic and household product must be checked for its potential to irritate human eyes and skin before it can be placed on the market. In the Draize test each chemical and household product is placed into the eyes of rabbits. Occasionally, the animals are restrained and given no anesthetics. Their eyes are examined over days and weeks to evaluate the damage, which can range from nothing to gross inflammation and alteration of the cornea. Public pressure has changed this practice, and at least in many cases the rabbits are now given local anesthetics to prevent pain during the application of substances that may be corrosive. Also, new methods are being developed using cultured human corneal cells, which show promise of being able to replace the Draize test for irritant substances.

These considerations place a moral burden on the granting agencies because one might question the use of cats, dogs, and rabbits, when rats and mice will suffice. Obviously people prefer the former species, but that is not the point nor does it justify being less concerned or humane to the smaller laboratory animals. I do not see a clear way out of this dilemma, except that granting agencies could be very specific in their guidelines, indicating that humane treatment of animals is equally applicable to all species.

However, guidelines are probably not enough. It may be necessary to conduct a campaign of public education to encourage humane treatment of all species used for experimentation at universities and in commercial laboratories. The latter use large numbers of small mammals, such as rabbits, rats, and mice, to satisfy Federal requirements and for a number of years have been rather casual about the ethical costs involved.

SUMMARY

In conclusion, I would like to stress that granting
agencies certainly have a responsibility for the welfare of
animals. Efforts have been made by NIH in this respect, and
several guidelines have been in effect for a number of years.
However, these guidelines could be more specific and perhaps
more forceful to prevent cruelty or misuse of animals.
The government, with good reason, has been careful not to
violate the privacy of investigators or their right to pursue
various avenues of research. Despite the difficulty and
importance of this issue, granting agencies can influence the
decisions of investigators by preventing the use of excessive
numbers of animals and by ensuring that those used for acute
experiments are properly treated to prevent pain. Also, they
can require that institutions provide better treatment of
animals used for chronic experimentation. In general, NIH
has made a concerted effort to protect the welfare of experimental animals within the framework of existing laws, which
may be equivocal at times. On the other hand, if laws become
too specific and restrictive, especially if they are proposed
by individuals not involved in animal experimentation, they
may have disastrous consequences for the future of biomedical
research.
As far as I am concerned, the ultimate solution rests
with the morality of the investigators involved in the various research projects. This has to be stressed through a
national campaign of public education, to make sure that
institutions receiving government funds have adequate facilities for the proper care and use of animals and that investigators responsible for the ultimate conduct of the research
have the proper credentials to perform these experiments.

FURTHER READING

For this presentation I have made use of the excellent
articles listed below. Citations from these papers were used
to further the thoughtful comments of the authors.

Schiller, J., Claude Bernard and vivisection, J. Hist. Med.
22, 246-260 (1967).

French, R. D., and Singer, P., Animal experimentation,
Encycl. of Bioethics 1, 75-83 (1978).

Rowan, A. N., The test tube alternative, The Sciences 21,
16-20 (1981).

RESPONSIBILITY OF FUNDING AGENCIES: CENTRAL OR LOCAL CONTROL?

David J. Ramsay

Department of Physiology
University of California School of Medicine
San Francisco, California

Joseph S. Spinelli

Animal Care Facility
University of California School of Medicine
San Francisco, California

The majority of research involving animals in the United States is financed with Federal dollars. Independent of which Federal agency is involved, distribution of these Federal dollars depends on prospective judgments of proposed experiments. Applicants submit grants that describe experiments they wish to carry out to test scientific hypotheses, and these are judged and ranked by a peer review system and supported according to the availability of funds. Two formal checks in the system ensure that the institution in which the research is to be carried out has the appropriate facilities for Animal care. The first check is provided under the auspices of the Animal Welfare Acts; the second depends upon a formal statement of adherence to the principles set out in the <u>Guide for the Care and Use of Laboratory Animals</u>, prepared by the Institute of Laboratory Animal Resources of the National Research Council.

The Animal Welfare Acts of 1966, 1970, and 1976, and the regulations of these Acts set out in Title IX require that any research facility using live, warm-blooded animals shall register with the Veterinary Services of the U.S. Department of Agriculture (USDA) in the State. Some animals, notably mice and rats, are specifically excluded from the definition of live, warm-blooded animals. Registration of a facility

acknowledges acceptance of standards which regulate the
purchase, handling, and humane care of animals used in
research. One important feature of registration is that an
annual report has to be submitted. This report contains not
only the number of animals that have been used in research,
but also responses to questions about experiments in which
pain or distress has accompanied the procedures and for which
anesthetic and analgesic agents were withheld because they
would have adversely affected the results of the experiments.
Provisions are also laid down for an institutional committee
(including a Doctor of Veterinary Medicine) to evaluate the
care, treatment, anesthesia, analgesia, and tranquilizing
procedures used in animals during research. Facilities which
are registered in this way are subjected to spot checks by
USDA inspectors. Thus, before grant money can be dispersed,
funding agencies are theoretically assured that the facilities are in compliance with the regulations of the Animal
Welfare Acts.

The National Institutes of Health (NIH) and other major
Federal suppliers of grant money for biomedical research have
a parallel system of regulations in the form of the Guide for
the Care and Use of Laboratory Animals. In this report, we
shall discuss the procedures used by NIH, the major funding
agency for biomedical research, but similar mechanisms are in
place by other funding agencies.

Any applicant organization for Public Health Service
(PHS) grants must assure NIH, in writing, that they are
committed to follow principles of animal care laid down in
the Guide. Such an assurance is lodged with the Office for
Protection from Research Risks (OPRR). Furthermore, the
institution must assure the PHS in writing that it has
established a review committee to assist in the fulfillment
of this commitment. No PHS award that involves the use of
animals can be made unless such assurances have been approved
by OPRR.

The research institution must either be accredited by the
American Association for Accreditation of Laboratory Animal
Care (AAALAC) or have an institutional committee that reviews
its animal facilities. The institutional committee is re-
sponsibile for lodging an annual report with OPRR that states
either that the facility is accreditable or attests to the
progress the research facility is making toward accreditable
status. Actually, the institutional committee required by
the Animal Welfare Acts is usually the same one required by
the PHS.

Thus, in practice, much of the overseeing of animal
experimentation is carried out at the level of the research
institution. A committee, often called the Animal Care
Committee, has to be assured that the standards of housing

and general husbandry of the animals conforms to the standards laid down in the Guide and in the Animal Welfare Acts. Methods of anesthesia, analgesia, and euthanasia have to be approved. If the experimental procedure is likely to cause greater distress than would normally accompany the administration of an anesthetic, the animals must first be rendered incapable of perceiving pain and must be maintained in that condition until the experiment or procedure is over. The only exception to this guideline is the case where the anesthetic would defeat the purpose of the experiment and where data cannot be obtained in any other way. Postoperative care of animals must be designed to minimize discomfort and has to be in accordance with acceptable practices in veterinary medicine. Thus, the local Animal Care Committee plays a most important role and is responsible for ensuring that research involving animals is carried out as humanely as possible.

In addition to this control at the local level, all who participate in the grant review process are alerted to be aware of animal welfare issues. This includes NIH staff and reviewers. If at any point in the review process a situation is identified which shows noncompliance with regulations, no grant can be awarded until the situation is clarified. In practice, the institutional Animal Care Committee is informed of the concern and will take steps to investigate the situation. However, until the Department of Health and Human Services is satisfied that there is compliance with the regulations, no award can be made.

Another way in which the funding agency can gain information is the site visit. Individuals on the site visit team can be specifically charged with looking into the physical facilities or finding out more details about the experimental procedures. The intent is that this system of local and Federal checks will assure that experimental procedures and animal handling are in compliance with the principles of the Guide and Animal Welfare Acts.

A question that may legitimately be raised is: how effective are these control mechanisms? Unannounced spot checks by USDA inspectors can pick up obvious infringements, such as overcrowding of animals in cages, unsanitary conditions, or inadequate ventilation. However, these visits occur too infrequently to be relied upon as the sole mechanism to ensure compliance. The same point can be made about Federal grant-giving bodies such as NIH. Although animal welfare issues concerning the nature of experiments can be addressed in the grant review process and the physical facilities can be inspected by a site visit team, it is likely that only gross infringements and inadequacies could be picked up in this way.

In a sense this is recognized by putting much of the
responsibility for regulating animal experimentation on the
Animal Care Committee at the institution where the research
is to be performed. As has been discussed earlier, under the
auspices of the Animal Welfare Acts, the local committee,
which includes a veterinarian, has jurisdiction over anesthesia, surgery, postoperative care, and general conduct of
the experiments. On the other hand, if an institution does
not have AAALAC accreditation, NIH, through its OPRR, requires an annual report on the physical facilities of the
animal care facility. Here again, when either the administrative staff or peer review committees are concerned about
an animal-related issue, the Animal Care Committee of the
institution is requested to check into the situation and make
recommendations to correct it. No grant can be awarded
unless NIH is satisfied with animal welfare issues. Thus, in
all these situations it is the local committee, rather than
central regulations, that exerts the most control.

In order to formalize this responsibility, many Animal
Care Committees are moving toward a review of grant proposals
before they are submitted. A number of factors have contributed to this development. First, the utility of such a
review process is suggested in the Acts. In recent years,
there has been a heightened public awareness of animal
welfare issues concerning the use of animals in research.
Scientists in the biomedical community are not immune from
this movement, and there has generally been increased sensitivity to such issues in the scientific community at large.
Finally, legislative efforts at both the State and Federal
level have suggested a compulsory review of grant proposals
by broadly based Animal Care Committees that might even
include members of the lay public. A number of institutions
have adopted a policy based on the Canadian model (and used
in some European countries), which also involves committee
screening for welfare issues.

Our own institution, through its Animal Care Committee,
adopted such a grant review process some 2 years ago. Every
grant, whether intra- or extramural, that involves the use of
animals has to go through this review process, similar to the
review of experiments involving humans by the Human Experimentation Committee. As our institution processes many
hundreds of grants each year, it would be impossible for our
Animal Care Committee to read every grant in detail. Therefore, to deal with the practicalities of the situation, those
applying for grants have to submit a Vertebrate Use Form to
the Animal Care Committee. This form requests information
about the number of animals used, the methods of anesthesia
and euthanasia, and details of experimental protocols. Each
form is first checked by one of the veterinarians attached to

the Animal Care Facility. Where the experiments are acute--
that is, where an animal will be anesthetized, an experiment
performed, and the animal euthanized before the end of the
experiment--if the veterinarian is satisfied with the method
of anesthesia and euthanasia, the form will not be reviewed
by the whole committee. On the other hand, all experiments
involving operation and survival and all those on conscious
animals are reviewed by the whole committee.

A practical point which at first caused concern was
whether this review would delay the process of submitting a
grant. Human nature being what it is, many grants are not
finished until a day or two before the submission deadlines.
This concern was overcome by allowing grants to go forward to
NIH as long as Vertebrate Use Forms had been submitted to the
committee. However, if a grant is awarded, the University
will not accept funding for that grant unless the approval of
the project by the Animal Care Committee has first been
received.

Experience of this process for the last 2 years has been
most encouraging. Most of the projects we review fully
satisfy all animal welfare issues. In situations where
problems are perceived by the committee, our usual practice
is to ask the investigator to come to a meeting to answer
questions about the project. We have been most gratified by
the cooperation such a process has engendered. The meeting
is not confrontational, and in all cases experiments have
been redesigned, very often around the table at the full
committee meeting, in ways which fully alleviated concerns on
animal welfare issues. It has been a rewarding experience.

An important offshoot of this process has been improved
communication between investigators, animal caretakers, and
veterinarians. The animal caretakers are the individuals
most directly concerned with day-to-day supervision of animals in the Animal Care Facility. Improved communication
between the faculty carrying out the experiments, the caretakers who look after the animals, and the veterinarian who
advises, can improve all aspects of animal welfare.

A problem which had to be dealt with was the extent to
which the review of welfare issues should take into account
the soundness of the science. We decided that the committee,
whose responsibility was to safeguard the care of animals,
should not undertake to comment on the science. The breadth
of the research subject matter covered in a large health-
sciences campus means there is no way that one committee
would have the competence to deal with it. Moreover, this
evaluation is the job of the peer review committee to which
the grant is submitted. We view the Animal Care Committee as
a place where knowledge and expertise in animal-related
issues should be developed, with the committee's observations

addressed simply to welfare aspects of animal experimentation. Thus, in many ways this is a parallel review process
avoiding unnecessary duplication of effort.

In this way, Federal grant-giving bodies solve their
responsibility with a mixture of central and local control.
Throughout the country local Animal Care Committees have
reached various levels of evolution. Do they provide
adequate protection? It is impossible to stand over each
experimenter every time the individual carries out an experiment. This system of regulation, as is true of many others,
involves trust. It is generally recognized that good biomedical science involves good animal models. Nothing of any
worth is achieved by using poor-quality animals, by having
poor husbandry, or by causing unnecessary stress to experimental animals.

The existing partnership in central and local control
should be further developed and refined. The responsibility
of the funding agencies should be to lay down a framework of
regulations which will assure the proper humane care of
animals involved in research. The system of local control,
where researchers themselves play an important role in carrying out regulations, is equally important. If the local
committee can heighten the sensitivities of all those involved in research to animal welfare issues, this is surely
the best way to minimize or end the abuse of laboratory
animals.

FUNDING AGENCY RESPONSIBILITIES
IN ANIMAL EXPERIMENTATION

Keith Kraner

Division of Research Grants
National Institutes of Health
Bethesda, Maryland

As the primary source of support for animal research in
the United States, the National Institutes of Health (NIH)
assumes a responsibility for humane and essential use of
animal subjects. The NIH addresses this responsibility at
several checkpoints.

One is the peer review process. Study Section members
are asked to include animal care concerns in their review of
grant applications. In addition to merit, applications are
judged on concerns such as use of the appropriate animal
model, use of the smallest number of animals to achieve the
experiment's goals, and protection of animal subjects from
unnecessary pain, stress, or discomfort. When deficiencies
are noted, Study Section members flag the proposals for
follow-up staff action.

A second checkpoint is the NIH's Guide for the Care and
Use of Laboratory Animals. This booklet was first published
in 1965 as a project of the National Research Council, whose
members are drawn from the National Academy of Sciences, the
National Academy of Engineering, and the Institute of Medicine. The booklet has been revised three times since then.
As the principal guide to the operation of laboratory facilities throughout the United States, the Guide sets standards
for appropriate housing, caging, feeding, and sanitation
practices. It also details a broad range of standards on
everything from temperature control and air changes of animal
facilities to training of animal care personnel. The NIH
requires each grantee institution to file a letter with the
Office for Protection from Research Risks stating that its
institutional animal facilities and programs of animal care
comply with the standards set up in the Guide.

SCIENTIFIC PERSPECTIVES ON ANIMAL WELFARE

Those grantee institutions that lack adequate animal facilities can apply to NIH for grants-in-aid. This program provides funds to assist grantees in upgrading their animal research facilities and programs. The grants-in-aid program also supplies funds for diagnostic laboratories to aid in disease control and health maintenance programs for research animals. In addition, NIH training program grants are available to educate veterinarians in the specialty of laboratory animal medicine.

A third checkpoint is either accreditation of the laboratory animal facilities by the American Association for Accreditation of Laboratory Animal and Care (AAALAC) or an annual inspection and status of compliance report by an institutional committee composed of at least five members experienced with animal research. One member must be a veterinarian.

I personally believe that the weakest link in the chain is the grantee institutional review committee's assurance that the animal facilities and programs of animal care are adequate. These committees are not standardized; they are set up on an ad hoc basis by each individual institution. Consequently, they range in quality across the country from excellent to almost ineffectual.

I propose two recommendations: (a) require all NIH grantee institutions to be either AAALAC-accredited or reviewed by a qualified outside committee at least every 2 years; and (b) require that all research applications involving animals be approved by an institutional animal use review committee before the application is submitted to NIH for funding. This review committee could be patterned after the Institutional Review Boards that currently operate for protection of human subjects.

SUMMARY OF WORKSHOP
ON FUNDING AGENCY RESPONSIBILITIES

F. Barbara Orlans[1]

National Institutes of Health
Bethesda, Maryland

A. Are Animal Issues Adequately Addressed During Preaward
Merit Review by Funding Agencies?

For background, it may be useful to describe some fairly
typical review procedures by public and private funding
agencies prior to award of a grant or contract. Funding
agencies are responsible for a critically important stage in
the total review process for quality animal experimentation.
Typically, they review animal experimentation procedures at
the same time as scientific merit. Experts in the scientific
area of the grant proposal usually meet as a committee to
discuss the proposals. The NIH Study Sections are an
example.
Among the animal issues that need to be addressed during
pre-award review by funding agencies are the following:

(1) Is the experiment scientifically meritorious and
relevant to improving human or animal health or to contributing to basic knowledge?
(2) Is the ethical cost of using the animal in balance
with the scientific significance of the expected results?
(3) Are animals really required to test this hypothesis?
If so, what are the proper species and numbers?

[1]This chairman's summary is a report of workshop discussions
and does not necessarily represent the views of the National
Institutes of Health.

SCIENTIFIC PERSPECTIVES ON ANIMAL WELFARE

The appropriateness of an animal procedure depends on the experience of the investigator with the proposed animal procedure, availability of the species to be used in the numbers required, adequacy of animal facilities, and timely termination of an experiment with proper methods of euthanasia. For projects involving invasive animal procedures, the provisions for minimizing pain and the adequacy of anesthesia, analgesia, and postprocedural care need to be assessed.

A number of funding agencies, including the American Heart Association and the NIH, specifically instruct their review committees to address animal concerns. Some agencies, however, do not issue any specific instructions; they just assume it will be done. Sensitivity to animal concerns might be enhanced if more funding agencies always gave such instructions.

Conferees agreed that the review of animal experimentation by funding agency committees does not always occur to the extent that it should. Few grant proposals are flagged for action on animal concerns. An NIH staff person reported that in a recent series of 1,240 consecutive NIH grant proposals, only 3 were identified by Study Sections for followup staff action because of animal welfare concerns. In the same series, 23 proposals were flagged for human experimentation concerns. Yet NIH funds more projects involving animals than human subjects. The question is posed whether all animal concerns are being adequately identified.

Other NIH staff members also reported anecdotally on their experiences. One said that out of 60 grant applications, just 1 was flagged for animal concerns. An Executive Secretary said that of 1,500 applications recently reviewed in his Study Section, none was refused on animal welfare concerns. This Study Section reviews some highly invasive animal procedures.

No one present at the workshop knew of comparable data from other Federal agencies, from any private funding organizations, or from industry. The relative number of grant applications that are identified for animal concerns in various review systems is a matter of conjecture. More information would be helpful.

Workshop participants noted that in some cases grant applications do not include adequate information on which proper assessment for animal concerns can be made. It was suggested that deficient applications be returned to the investigator for additional information. It appeared this was done sometimes but perhaps not often enough.

As noted previously, in most systems one committee reviews both for scientific merit and animal concerns. Often committee members are chosen solely for their expertise in the appropriate scientific discipline. Rarely are they

chosen specifically for expertise in animal concerns. Therefore, a problem with some funding agency review committees is
that members lack experience in addressing animal experimentation concerns. This could be corrected by appropriate
education at many different levels. The usefulness of
involving large numbers of investigators in the review experience, at both the institutional and central funding agency
levels, was commented upon. More training to enhance sensitivity to animal concerns was recommended.

A different system has been used by the Veterans Administration (VA). Here, one committee reviews for animal concerns, and then subsequently another committee reviews for
scientific merit. The scientific merit committee has the
benefit of the comments from the previous review. The VA
system provides a more thorough review for animal concerns
than other known systems. The VA special committees, for
instance, not infrequently return an application to an investigator for additional information. Conferees familiar with
the VA system commented favorably on it and cited it as a
model for other funding agencies to follow.

Recommendations. Inasmuch as there is general agreement
that proper care and use of experimental animals is desirable, it was recommended:

(1) That funding agencies require investigators applying
for grants to specifically address animal issues. Such
documentation would provide necessary information to the
reviewers, so that they can discharge their function of
reviewing proposals for proper treatment of animals.

(2) That public and private funding agencies use
consultants with expertise in animal issues to review
selected grant proposals that pose special concerns.
Initially, such consultants could serve as ad hoc review
panel members. Eventually, some funding organizations may
find it appropriate to establish entire committees composed
of such consultants, as is done currently by the Veterans
Administration.

(3) That workshops and training courses be provided on
how to review scientific proposals for animal welfare issues.
Executive Secretaries and present and future members of
funding agency review committees, as well as graduate students, technicians, ethicists, and community representatives,
could benefit from such continuing education. Training
should be provided in the type of decision-making reviewers
are called upon to do.

This could be done most usefully perhaps with case
studies based on situations that have actually occurred.

Similar educational instruction has been developed and is
being used to train people to work effectively on human
investigation review committees. In these case studies,
varying viewpoints are described, along with recommendations
for modifications of the protocol to make it acceptable.
Where the protocol was disallowed, the reasons for this
decision would be detailed.

(4) That a prospective evaluation be made of peer review
systems for animal welfare concerns. Evaluation could be
made, for instance, of the frequency with which animal welfare concerns are identified by public and private funding
agency review panels and institutional Animal Care and Use
Committees, and followup actions could be documented. The
purpose would be to show the impact of new measures now being
enacted.

(5) That present policies be reassessed to see if
additional requirements would be beneficial to ensure high
standards of humane animal care.

B. Should Funding Agencies Make Selected Site Visits?

It was generally agreed that random site visits to
examine animal facilities and the operations of institutional
committees are beneficial. The teams must include persons
with special expertise in laboratory animal medicine, and the
visits should be made not only to recipients of large center
grants with significant animal usage, but also to others on a
random basis, and to institutions with a history of inadequate or marginal animal care. In October 1981, NIH publicly
announced that it would start to implement spot site visits
to review animal experimentation procedures and animal facilities at funded institutions. Strong endorsement was voiced
at the workshop for such site visits.

In general, the only site visit for animal concerns that
an institution currently receives is when accreditation for
the animal facility is sought. The accrediting body is the
American Association for Accreditation of Laboratory Animal
Care (AAALAC). In 1981 about 30 percent of U.S. research
institutions were accredited by AAALAC. Several workshop
participants suggested that funding agencies should encourage
more institutions to become AAALAC-accredited. Also it was
suggested that the roster of AAALAC reviewers could be made
available to funding agencies for use as animal experts, as
needed.

Several years ago the VA ordered that all VA centers
using animals be accredited, thus becoming the nation's
leader in such accreditation. Many participants believed
that funding agencies should make awards contingent upon

AAALAC or equivalent accreditation of the facility. It was recognized that some appropriate lead time must be given for compliance, for example, 5 years. An acceptable alternative, for those who elect otherwise, would be to submit to outside review by qualified experts.

Recommendations. It was recommended that:

(1) Spot visits should be encouraged by funding agencies specifically to assess animal welfare concerns. These site visits must include persons with special expertise in laboratory animal medicine.

(2) Greater emphasis should be placed on AAALAC accreditation or equivalent outside review of animal facilities.

C. In What Manner Should Institutional Animal Care and Use Committees Be Accountable to Funding Agencies?

A number of conference participants had experience in serving on institutional Animal Care and Use Committees, either as chairpersons or as members. They expressed some interesting viewpoints based on this experience.

In the first place, it was pointed out that not all institutions have such committees. No data were available regarding the overall frequency of such committees or the type of institution most likely to have such a committee. Furthermore, even where such a committee exists, it does not necessarily function in a meaningful manner. The workshop discussion highlighted the need for a national survey on the distribution and functioning of these committees.

It was the consensus of the group that funding agencies should require institutional review of research proposals before funding. This places primary emphasis where it should be--at the institutional level.

Funding agencies also should require certain standards of institutional Animal Care and Use Committees. For instance, a requirement can be made concerning the composition of the committees. Institutional Committees commonly consist of research investigators. Sometimes these are the only members, and sometimes they review their own or their colleagues' work. This was judged inadequate. Critical evaluation is lacking where conflict of interest exists. Persons with conflict of interest should be excluded from participating in that review.

Broad representation of many viewpoints is essential for effective functioning of these committees. Perhaps surprisingly, a unanimous consensus emerged that local committees

should include animal or laboratory technicians in addition
to research investigators. Technicians provide a unique
viewpoint not represented by any other group of persons.
They are the ones most intimately involved with the animals.
They frequently prepare the animal for the experimental
procedure and personally tend the animal postoperatively.
Their judgment of the adequacy of animal care is invaluable.
Furthermore, technicians are not inhibited by peer loyalty or
other pressures to remain silent if they see anything that
requires remedial action.

Some conferees reported favorably on the use of
technicians on their institutional committees. They urged
wider acceptance of this practice. The Swedish system of
requiring that one-third of the committee membership be
technicians was cited (see Professor Öbrink's article).

Another unanimous consensus was that graduate students
serve as members of institutional committees. This would
provide the students with invaluable review experience and
would sensitize them to animal welfare concerns. This
practice would help to build for future, responsible
decision-making.

The majority, with some dissenters, also agreed that
members of the lay community should serve on institutional
committees. Several participants indicated that this is
already being done at their institutions. The community
member might be an ethicist. The best way is for each
locality to decide what works best for them. Flexibility was
recommended to accommodate local differences.

Accountability of institutional committees to the funding
agency could be enhanced by certain other requirements,
including recordkeeping. Documentation should be kept, for
instance, of the number of times the institutional committee
meets each year, the minutes of the meetings, the types of
animal problems identified, the actions taken, and the appropriate followup. Several workshop participants said that
requiring more documentation was acceptable but that submitting a volume of paper to the funding agency was not. No
one wanted to increase the files of unread papers. Appropriate documentation of the committee's deliberations should
be maintained by the institution. It should be available for
spot checks by the funding agency on request.

It was strongly advocated that funding agencies use their
influence more effectively. They can apply needed pressure
on institutions to require compliance with appropriate animal
care and use standards. The threat of withholding funds from
institutions not in compliance would provide effective
leverage to convince institutions to assign a high priority
to this effort. The prestige of institutional Animal Care

and Use Committees would benefit from more stringent requirements.

Furthermore, if funding agencies made greater demands, institutions would allocate more resources toward animal welfare measures. Resources are needed to run effective Animal Care and Use Committees, to hire and train appropriate personnel to care for the animals, and to upgrade animal equipment and facilities. It is currently difficult to obtain institutional support for such expenditures because of competing demands.

Funding agency support for improving animal facilities may not be adequate. For instance, it was noted that the current NIH program for upgrading animal facilities to bring them into compliance with federally mandated standards had been cut back. Only $300,000 were allocated for this purpose in FY 1981. By comparison, in FY 1974 over $3 million had been awarded in this program. No data were available regarding other Federal or private funding agency allocations for this purpose.

Recommendations. It was recommended that:

(1) Research protocols should be reviewed by the institutions' Animal Care and Use Committees before submission to funding agencies (also see comments on this topic in Section II).

(2) Funding agencies should encourage institutional Animal Care and Use Committees to conform to certain standards. Memberships on the committees should provide for balanced and broad representation of viewpoints, free from conflict of interest. Opinion should be solicited from animal technicians, laboratory technicians, graduate students, and community representatives, wherever possible.

(3) Funding agencies could, with benefit, require institutional committees to keep records of their deliberations, which could be open for inspection upon request. Institutional committees could be required to meet a minimum number of times each year.

By requiring these three types of accountability, the funding agencies could enhance the effectiveness of animal welfare policies.

SECTION IV

EDITORIAL RESPONSIBILITIES
IN ANIMAL EXPERIMENTATION

EDITORIAL RESPONSIBILITIES IN ANIMAL RESEARCH

Frank B. Golley

Institute of Ecology
University of Georgia
Athens, Georgia

The object of this paper is to explore how editorial
responsibility can be used to influence and control ethical
behavior in science. We shall focus on scientists' relationships with experimental animals.
One can view scientific activity as a sequential process
which is made up of a series of linked events, such as
exploration, discovery, test of hypothesis, communication,
and so forth. There are a variety of controls operating on
the sequence, regulating the direction and rate of advance.
These controls may be external or internal to the sequence.
That is, control may come either from outside or from inside
the scientific process and the institution. External control
might require that the research fit a regulation, fulfill
some norm, or accomplish a particular goal. Thus external
controls may be through legal regulation or economic or peer-
group pressure. In contrast, internal controls are moral,
ethical, and social rules which are part of the scientists'
code of behavior. Internal rules are formally taught or are
informally learned by imitation and discussion. Scientists
may draw up codes of behavior. In pure research that is not
a common approach, but applied scientists frequently have
codes which regulate their behavior within defined areas of
responsibility.
It is difficult to separate external from internal
control functions in any specific case because both operate
in the usual research program. Nevertheless, where ethical
questions are raised, it is necessary to attempt to make this
separation, because frequently the public seeks to transfer
control from the internal realm to the external and employ
the power of the state to ensure conformity with the publicly
approved behavior.

SCIENTIFIC PERSPECTIVES ON ANIMAL WELFARE

The question I've been asked to address here is the
effectiveness of editorial control to enforce acceptable
standards of behavior toward experimental or captive animals.
Of course, the question is raised because various publics
have expressed an opinion that rights of animals might be
abridged in some forms of scientific research. These publics
have proposed that the government establish regulations
setting appropriate standards of care and treatment of
captive animals and that the police power of the state be
used to assure that these regulations are enforced. Scientists have frequently drawn attention to the fact that
external regulation of science by nonscientific authorities
limits flexibility and opportunity. I suspect that most
scientists would be opposed to further formal regulation of
research. Clearly, it is useful to determine whether control
procedures natural to and internal to science could ensure
that public standards of behavior will be observed.
Scientific publication is one such point of control.

PUBLISHING AS A CONTROL PROCESS

The process of publication usually begins with the
submission of a manuscript to the editorial office of a
journal. This manuscript is read and evaluated by the
journal editor, by several editors, and/or by anonymous
reviewers. The paper usually follows a rigid format which
includes an introduction, a description of methods, results,
discussion of the significance of the results, and references
to other work used in the report. The writing style is also
relatively stereotyped, especially within a subdiscipline.
As a consequence editors can rather quickly determine whether
a paper has the accepted format and style and can concentrate
their attention on the relation of the results to advancement
of the field, on coherence with other results, on complete-
ness and logical development, and similar matters. While
some papers have fundamental faults in format, style, and
logical development, papers are more frequently rejected
because they are incomplete, do not add to the advancement of
the subject, or are inappropriate for the journal. Rejection
rates for the more prestigious journals are frequently 50 to
70 percent of all manuscripts received.
    Methods of research are usually not described in detail
in a scientific paper. Space is limited, and most writers
would rather use the available space to describe and discuss
research results. Frequently, methods are merely cited as
following those used in another earlier paper or those of

another worker. In addition, it is often difficult to recon-
struct the methods used in a study from the terse description
provided, especially if the reader is not familiar with the
specific topic or field of work. For these reasons it is
difficult for an editor or reviewer to determine how subject
animals have been used in an experiment, how they have been
maintained, and whether the work was done under standard
canons of ethical behavior.

Editorial responsibility alone seems to me a rather
ineffective point to control behavior. The omission of
relevant detail is so easy that the editor must usually take
a neutral position about animal welfare. I suspect that in
those few cases where ethical problems occur, the situation
becomes known through individuals associated with the project, who "blow the whistle" on an associate. In large,
complex research projects even the author of the paper may
not personally know how the experimental animals are maintained or treated. This part of the study may be carried out
by other departments or by associates, and the author may
deal only with quantitative data. Such authors would be ill-
equipped to discuss how experimental subjects were treated.

IMPROVEMENT OF THE SYSTEM

If we assume that the publication control point is a
desirable place to evaluate and apply standards of ethical
conduct, how can the publication process be changed so that
it is an effective control?

I believe that there are two major ways a change can be
accomplished. First, researchers using animals could be
required to make explicit in their publication the methods
employed in treating subjects. The editor then would have
adequate information upon which to make a judgment. But I
doubt that this approach would work. It would be difficult
to determine what has been omitted from a description of
methods or to determine what is an adequate and acceptable
description. It would penalize the vast majority of authors
who are ethical and would likely miss those few who are
unethical. Second, editors may be admonished, or even required, to consider animal welfare in their evaluation of
research papers. I suspect that most editors feel that they
presently consider animal welfare in evaluation of manuscripts and that a formal requirement would be of no material
help.

Therefore, while formal and informal controls at the
point of publication might be improved, I feel that publication is not an effective point of control by itself.

Rather, I suggest that evaluation of research proposals is a
much better point to exert control over methodology and,
together with editorial control, might be adequate to achieve
animal welfare objectives.

The research proposal usually must focus on methodology,
since the success of research depends partly on the methods
used in the study. These descriptions of methods are frequently full and are discussed in detail by reviewers and
panels. Not only are the protocols made explicit, but statements on costs, personnel needs, equipment, and supplies all
provide further insight into how the research will be conducted. This is an effective point to control research
procedures, and investigators are often willing to describe
the methods in additional detail or to modify methods
according to the reviewer's comments.

In the National Science Foundation (NSF), during my
tenure as Division Director of Environmental Biology, I heard
hundreds of discussions of research methodology in proposals,
and in a few cases I heard comments about the proposed treatment of experimental animals. While I believe that there are
relatively few cases where unethical behavior occurs, I am
impressed with how an effective peer review system, such as
that employed in the NSF Directorate of Biological, Behavior,
and Social Science, can detect abuse and correct it or judge
against it. If we must resort to external control for
ethical behavior, this is the most effective point in the
sequence, in my opinion.

INTERNAL CONTROLS

However, animal welfare, like any other ethical problem,
probably can best be regulated through internal controls in
the individual or in the research group. Internal controls
are frequently not explicit; they represent the "proper" or
the "correct" way to act in a given situation. The biolo-
gist's attitude toward animals is shaped by family and school
experiences, by having pets as a child, by the type of basic
biology courses one took in high school and college, and by
the attitudes of one's professional colleagues in graduate
school. Where the rights of animals are discussed in a
biological research context, the young research worker has a
different perception of ethical behavior from one where
animals are considered tools to achieve research results.

In my opinion the animal welfare issue is part of a
larger social problem in our society. This problem concerns
conscious or unconscious misuse and mistreatment of the
environment, other living beings, and other human beings. It

involves a focus on maximization of individual goals and a disregard of social and group goals and needs. It is represented by a self-centered, materialistic personality. It regards other living beings as things and is uninterested in maintenance of networks and complex relationships. It sacrifices means for ends, and it justifies unethical behavior by culturally accepted myths.

For individuals with such a world view, animal subjects become means toward ends. The end is narrowly conceived and/or is conceived as an isolated event. Frequently, mistreatment of the subjects is justified by a so-called improvement in human health or well-being. But this argument--the notion that one can injure, cause pain to, or kill an animal so that human life may be prolonged or improved--neglects the question of the value of life in general and of human life in particular. It ignores the fact that mistreatment of one being by another corrupts and diminishes the results of the study and ultimately creates more serious problems.

There is no question that species use, kill, and consume other species. The food chains of ecosystems provide vivid evidence of these relationships. However, predation and parasitism involve balanced relationships; they exist and have meaning only in the context of balance. Predation out of control results in the eventual demise of the predator. The coevolved systems of organisms are intricate and dynamic. Balance is not static, but rather is a continually shifting, growing, changing set of relationships, which only in retrospect appear static to the observer.

The problem for man is to recreate, encourage, and improve these relationships, especially the sense of living networks between men and between men and other forms of life. Man has in the past and can in the future create sociocultural systems which are symbiotic with nature, where life is recognized as a unique property to be respected and treasured, and where the value and quality of a relationship is recognized as being influenced by the quality of all other relationships.

The challenge for modern society is to use the vast wealth made possible by scientific research to improve the quality of symbiotic life on the earth. In this context man can take a moral and ethical position, sanctioned socially and culturally, to reduce imbalances in the flow of energy, materials, and information, thus reducing the oscillation in the world ecosystem and preserving life, even while recognizing that hierarchies of organization, heterogeneity in resource allocation, aggressive behavior, extinction, and death are operative now and will be in the future. This task is immensely more difficult than mere development of a

utopian social organization or five-year plan or religious
revival. The nature of this problem is made visible in the
animal welfare issue, and it creates an opportunity for
biologists to think about, discuss, and teach ethical concepts relating to animal life and man's relation to animals.

I believe that it is remarkable that the animal welfare
problem is so limited and restricted in place. One might
expect mistreatment of research animals to be as widespread
as the mistreatment of horses in the days of horse transport.
Yet I know very few instances of unethical behavior of this
sort among scientists. Science has operated with remarkably
ethical norms, quite separate from those of the larger society. As science becomes more open, these special attributes
will probably change. While change has been relatively slow,
we should not be complacent. Those of us concerned about
ethical behavior in science and society must continue to
analyze and understand controls in society, so that we can
propose and support acceptable controls which will encourage
and reward ethical behavior, without retarding or significantly limiting scientific progress.

EDITORIAL POLICY FOR ANIMAL EXPERIMENTATION

Garth J. Thomas

Center for Brain Research
University of Rochester Medical Center
Rochester, New York

I am just completing a 6-year stint as editor of the
Journal of Comparative and Physiological Psychology   (JCPP).
It is a society journal, i.e., it is a publication, along
with some 16 other publications, of the American Psychological Association (APA).
From my experience as editor of JCPP, I conclude that,
really, editors can do very little in the way of hard-nosed
enforcement of idiosyncratic notions of what constitutes
"welfare" for animal subjects. The notions of the requirements for the welfare of animal subjects grow as knowledge
grows. In addition they vary from time to time as the
political forces shift, which represent shifts in opinion and
values, not an increase in knowledge.
When I started my editorship, I wrote an editorial about
journal policy matters. One of the points I made was that it
would be grounds for rejecting a paper if the procedures
deviated from the American Psychological Association's code
of ethics regarding treatment and care of laboratory animals.
Incidentally, the code is very like that of the American
Physiological Society. In addition, I spoke explicitly of
three types of mistreatment of animals that have become
apparent only within the last few decades.
With regard to one of those problems--one with a long
history-- I simply proscribed the use of curare-like drugs as
an anesthetic. These drugs paralyze an organism by blocking
transmission at the neuromuscular junction. Such drugged
animals appear unresponsive to painful stimuli, so in the
early days many people took for granted that curare was an
anesthetic. Over the years since World War II, it has become
common knowledge that these drugs do not block sensory input.

They largely block motor outflow at the periphery--the neuromuscular junction. So even though the drugged animal is not
responsive, it is not anesthetized. I have not seen a paper
in recent years where curare-like drugs were treated (in
experimental procedures) as anesthetics. Nonetheless, I said
in my editorial that such papers would be rejected out of
hand.

Another problem concerns the use of restraining chairs
for primates. It has become apparent that some forms of
restraint, particularly of the back legs, if maintained for
long periods of time, can lead to pressure-point sores,
muscular weakness, and even paralysis. There are ways to
restrain monkeys, as is necessary for some experimental
problems, without injury or even undue discomfort to the
animal. A related problem concerns immobilization of the
head, which is necessary for some neurophysiologic studies
with chronically implanted brain electrodes. The monkey
chairs sometimes have what are called military collars to
hold the monkey's head up. They are uncomfortable, and if an
animal is left so restrained for some time, they can lead to
injuries.

A third problem concerns chronic electric stimulation of
the brain. When the stimulating electrode is in a system of
pain-conducting fibers or in a brain nucleus which processes
peripheral pain sensations, stimulation (especially in the
brain stem) can lead to excruciatingly painful sensations.

None of these procedures are specifically mentioned in
the APA's code of ethics, so in my editorial I proscribed
them. This position must already have been accepted by the
relevant scientists, or else the editorial was effective in
scaring them off from trying to publish in JCPP, because I
never received one manuscript that was in any way questionable with regard to these points.

I conclude that editors of relevant scientific journals
really can do very little in consciousness-raising with
regard to problems of animal welfare. They can codify
knowledge of procedures that are already well understood by
their scientific community. In the case of professional
societies which maintain codes of ethics relevant to the
problem and which have active ethics committees, the editor
can refer flagrant cases for the committee's consideration.
The most serious sanction they have is to eject the culprit
from the society, which of course can have very serious
consequences for the offender--or no consequences at all.

That's why I started this paper with the assertion that,
in my opinion, editors can do very little beyond codifying
already widely accepted beliefs in the relevant scientific
community.

EDITORIAL RESPONSIBILITIES IN THE CARE
AND MANAGEMENT OF ANIMALS
USED IN RESEARCH

Robert M. Berne

Department of Physiology
University of Virginia School of Medicine
Charlottesville, Virginia

The individuals involved in publication of scientific research--such as journal editors, associate and assistant editors, reviewers of manuscripts, and societies or groups who publish journals and provide suitable guidelines for animal care in research--are the last line of defense in protecting animals used in research from improper treatment and unnecessary pain or anxiety.

The first step in this process is often taken by the journal in providing guidelines promulgated by the National Institutes of Health for the care and treatment of animals used in research. These guidelines are clearly printed toward the front or back of each issue or in issues containing Instructions to Authors.

The second step is to require the reviewer to check a box on the review sheet that states that the experiments conform to the research animal guidelines as printed in the journal. In the event that the reviewer feels there is a violation, or if the reviewer has some doubts about the manner in which the animal experiments were conducted, he or she should either reject the paper, clearly stating the reason for the rejection, or require the author to provide additional information and clarification. Before the paper is accepted, it should be determined without question that the criteria for proper use of animals have been met.

The third step is for the editor(s) to check each manuscript to be certain that the reviewer did not overlook some violation of the research animal guidelines. The editor can then make a final judgment about acceptability, based on the reviewer's evaluation as well as his own. If the editor

SCIENTIFIC PERSPECTIVES ON ANIMAL WELFARE

still has some doubts, he or she can refer the dispute to the
animal care review committee of the society or group that
sponsors the journal. In cases of flagrant or repeated
violations, it would be appropriate for the editor to call
them to the attention of the author's departmental chairman
and possibly to his or her dean.

Finally, the editor, by means of an editorial or in the
instructions to authors, should encourage readers to inform
him or her of possible infractions of the rules and guidelines in the treatment of animals in research in published
papers.

Some cases of improper use of animals in research involve
the use of paralytic agents without documentation of adequate
anesthesia, the use of anesthetized versus unanesthetized
animals, or experiments involving such phenomena as shock,
trauma, burns, and noxious conditioning stimuli. Here one
must carefully weigh the value of the scientific research
versus the physical and emotional impact on the experimental
animal. The reviewer and editor must carefully estimate
whether the discomfort inflicted is worth the results, which
could prove to be of great benefit to humans. This is an
extremely difficult decision to make, but in the final
analysis it falls on the shoulders of the editor and his
advisory animal care committee.

The problems of proper animal use in research are very
difficult to resolve, since personal judgment is so intimately involved. Individuals, however compassionate and
knowledgeable, might easily give conflicting views on a given
problem. Nevertheless, every attempt should be made to
prevent ill treatment of animals used in research; and
although we may not be able to eliminate the problem completely, editorial review can serve a very useful function in
reducing to a minimum the number of violations that are
permitted to be published or pass unrecognized through the
review process. Of course, such review of manuscripts cannot
prevent improper animal experimentation. But it can prevent
publication; and with an appropriate admonition accompanying
the letter of rejection, it may discourage the investigator
from carrying out other experiments that are not in total
agreement with the animal care guidelines.

A number of scientific journals adhere to these policies
and, in general, are successful in screening out improper
animal utilization. Even under the closest scrutiny, however, some articles involving poor or inadequate animal care
in experimentation slip through. The only antidote is
greater vigilance on the part of reviewers and editors.
Hopefully, scientists, institutions, and granting agencies
will have a greater impact at an earlier stage in the development of research projects which will conform to animal care

guidelines. This kind of commitment not only makes the task of the editorial reviewers a bit easier, but also underscores the importance of maintaining proper standards for the use of animals in biomedical research to ensure continuing progress in our efforts to combat human disease.

SUMMARY OF WORKSHOP
ON EDITORIAL RESPONSIBILITIES

Michael W. Fox

Institute for the Study of Animal Problems
Washington, District of Columbia

A. How Can Editorial Policy Assure Humane Use of Animals in Research?

It was generally agreed that the final point of animal welfare insurance is at the editorial level, where a research paper may be rejected, not on scientific quality, but for improper regard for the animals' welfare or for the inappropriateness of the animal model. Editorial vetoes will help to inhibit future irresponsibility, although it was emphasized that many inferior journals accept any and all papers and have no review process.

Recommendations. The editor's task of welfare assessment can be enhanced by:

1. The journal publishing guidelines for the welfare of experimental animals (e.g., American Journal of Physiology).
2. Requiring a statement, signed by the investigator and the institution's veterinarian or other representative of the Animal Care and Use Committee, confirming that existing welfare codes and laws were adhered to (e.g., Journal of the American Heart Association).
3. Having reviewers assist editors in appraising submitted papers for adherence to animal welfare standards (in addition to scientific merit), provided the reviewers are fully informed as to the appropriate animal welfare codes.
4. Having an oversight committee on animal welfare or a laboratory animal scientist determine whether a manuscript should be accepted or rejected when it has high scientific

merit but ethical concerns are raised about the animal studies. The reason for any rejection on the basis of welfare concerns should be communicated in detail to the investigator, to the institution's Director of Animal Facilities, to the Animal Care and Use Committee, and/or to other appropriate responsible authority.

5.   Having a numerical classification, based on the degree of intervention and physical or psychological trauma, which would help focus more attention on manuscripts with a high degree of invasive experimentation (see Professor Öbrink's article for such a classification).

6.   Having the experimental protocol and methodology published in detail for manuscripts in general--and especially for those with a high numerical rating for invasiveness.   Such publication (possibly in small print to economize on space) would help allay the concerns of persons interested in animal welfare whose primary access to what goes on in research laboratories is through journal articles.

7.   Requesting that the purpose of the study be clearly stated in the introduction. The seeming absence of a clear purpose or justification is another reason why individuals concerned with animal welfare have a clouded and often negative regard for many scientific articles.

8.   Establishing codes of practice expressing each journal's editorial policy with reference to humane guidelines for animal care during experimentation (use of analgesics and restraint procedures; minimization of unnecessary pain, fear, anxiety, or deprivation). The Council of Biological Editors could be instrumental by endorsing the principles of such codes.

This would improve the quality of research, since good animal care often equates with good science. It would also help to ensure scientific and journal accountability and responsibility to the public, thus enhancing the public image of biomedical research on animals.   It may also protect journals from the threat of lawsuits over unethical or inhumane research conducted by investigators who have falsely claimed to have adhered to proper guidelines.

Good editorial review of scientific papers should address not only the quality, validity, and relevance of the research, but also the quality and extent of animal care. A balance should be sought between scientific advances and ethical costs, so that neither scientific progress and freedom nor accountability will be jeopardized.

SECTION V
PUBLIC POLICY AND RECOMMENDATIONS

THE RESPONSIBILITY OF SCIENTISTS IN DETERMINATION OF PUBLIC POLICY FOR THE USE OF ANIMALS IN BIOMEDICAL RESEARCH

Harlyn O. Halvorson

Rosenstiel Basic Medical Sciences Research Center
Brandeis University
Waltham, Massachusetts

At a conference on "Social and Ethical Implications of Science and Technology," Professor Barnard Barber of Columbia University argued that because science is inescapably a part of the social and political process, scientists have every right to defend and advance scientific values and interests in a manner consistent with the democratic process (1). In doing so, however, scientists must respect other societal values and interests. Because current scientific institutions are ill-equipped to deal with these societal questions, the scientific community must form new institutions for this purpose.

The Scientists Center for Animal Welfare has recognized this challenge in sponsoring this "First Conference on Scientific Perspectives in Animal Welfare." While historically the issues are neither novel nor new, I applaud the stated intent that scientists take the initiative for fostering responsible use of animals in experimentation. This meeting has a broad coverage, which has included the responsibilities of government, institutions, and individuals for animal experimentation; the responsibilities of editors of journals and of funding agencies--collectively these responsibilities govern experimental design--and, although not explicitly stated, the responsibility of the public. The issues are complex. The participants extend from the concerned scientist to the dedicated scientist, and the prospects depend upon the efficient use of limited Federal resources in a climate of increased accountability for public expenditures.

This is an important forum. The future of biomedical
research--and with it, the public health and welfare--is
dependent upon a climate of general understanding. It is
axiomatic that this cannot be achieved unless all parties
concerned are involved. Since the issues addressed by this
conference have broad parallels in other areas of public
policy in science, it is appropriate to draw upon other
public experience in facing the questions of animal research
in the coming decade.

ROLE OF INDIVIDUAL SCIENTISTS AND SCIENTIFIC SOCIETIES

Should individual scientists assume a social responsibility for determining research policies? I would answer
strongly in the affirmative. There is a historic precedent
for such a response. Since World War II, we have modern
evidence of such responsibility by individual scientists.
First, following the use of atomic bombs in World War II,
physicists lost their innocence, took active roles in public
debate, and formed a journal, the Bulletin of Atomic Scientists, to exchange views. Some 25 to 30 years later the same
loss of innocence occurred with biologists. This loss has
been associated with increasing use of hazardous compounds,
human experimentation, the abusive use of antibiotics, regulation of recombinant DNA, and the use of animals in research. As further evidence for social responsibility,
scientists have formed committees of concerned scientists,
organizations such as Science for the People, environmental-
oriented organizations, and coalitions of professional organizations to support their views.
       Professional scientific societies have also played an
important role. They provide the instrument for debating the
issues, collecting the necessary expertise, and supplying the
public and its representatives with all relevant facts and
uncertainties in a responsible manner. Scientific societies
have both the interest and moral obligation to speak out on
matters where their scientific expertise is required for
evaluation of the issues. They have created public affairs
committees and ethics committees and have sponsored numerous
conferences on science and ethics.
       In addition, scientific journals are increasingly filled
with letters to the editor and debates on issues involving
ethical questions. Nationally, the Commission on Human
Consent and an Office for Science and Technology Policy were
established. Scientists have also participated widely in
risk assessment surveys and the shaping of regulations and
legislation. The evidence for the role of scientists in

today's social responsibilities is clearly evident, and the need for their participation is increasing.

PUBLIC IMAGE OF SCIENCE

Modern problems are complex and require careful analysis by respected experts. John Sawhill, former president of New York University, said several years ago: "I am not impressed by recent polls purporting to show that in the American public opinion, science and its practitioners are as hallowed as ever. Scientists may consistently rank higher in public esteem than ministers, architects, lawyers, bankers, and congressmen, but from what I have observed on the college campus and in the classroom, faith in the beneficence of scientific endeavor and the promise of technology has been steadily eroding." (2)

Some of the reasons for today's more jaundiced view of science are obvious, others less so. Scientists have been the bearers of bad news in recent years, and bad tidings rarely enhance the popularity of those who deliver them.

People do not comprehend the often circuitous paths to scientific discovery. Many people do not understand why men and women should be paid for studying the mating habits of spiders and the sonar systems of bats when the planet itself seems to be in peril.

In May, 1981, Dr. Derek Bok president of Harvard University, in speaking of the morale of science, wrote: "Even so, one cannot be complacent about the morale of American science, for the sources of criticism and self-doubt clearly are greater today than they were 50 years, or even 25 years ago. One element of concern is surely the rapid growth of public skepticism about the benefits of science--or more precisely, of technology and innovation. Another is the conviction, by now widespread, that knowledge is not neutral and that investigators must take greater responsibility for the social consequences of their research." (3)

The growing cynicism about science must be tackled at its roots through better scientific education. People must be taught the limits as well as the possibilities of science and, most important, its changing and vastly enlarged role in our national and global destiny.

In my opinion the question is not whether individual scientists bear social responsibility, but the proper role in which that responsibility is to be expressed. Dr. Philip Handler (4), past president of the National Academy of Sciences, has pointed out, as have others recently, that for the first time in recent history in this country we are in a

negative technology balance. That is, fewer patents are
being produced in this country than are being bought from
outside the country, and we are importing more technology
than we are exporting. Since technology is based upon new,
fundamental information from basic science, a continual flow
of basic science to technology is essential to maintaining
our modern society. In this process scientists have an
important role to play.

CONTRIBUTIONS OF BASIC SCIENCE

In a recent book on Biomedical Scientists and Public
Policy, Lewis Thomas (5), one of our most effective spokesmen
for science, argued that science is good for the human mind
and is as important for the development of collective human
thought as any of the forms of art that seek meaning. Use of
science involves an anlysis of risks versus benefits. Three
major benefits can be identified. The first is a more comprehensive understanding of nature--the enrichment of the
human spirit. The second involves information that can be
used to solve major human problems in the future; this is
particularly true regarding human disease. The third involves information that can be put directly to use for practical or beneficial programs.
      One of the major dilemmas that we have had in our society
has been the attempt to make distinctions between basic and
applied science. These distinctions can often cause more
difficulties than provide useful definitions. This is particularly true when we deal with the problem of science
planning. At one extreme, applied science involves endeavors
where one has a large body of scientific information that
comprises an orderly and abundant array of indsputable facts.
Given this body of information, one can design teams of experts who can evaluate and coordinate basic plans to exploit
these facts for highly predictable, profitable utilization.
The Apollo program was one example, as was the development of
the Salk vaccine and whole-body scanners, which earned Nobel
Prizes a few years ago. This research is generally very
expensive.
      At the other extreme, with research involving basic
science, we are dealing with a very high degree of uncer-
tainty. The individual scientist is looking for new facts to
fit into a mechanism or to explain a new idea. New information is a surprise rather than a prediction, and the research
is relatively inexpensive. Such ventures are not easily
planned. They are not subject to readily adopted management
procedures.

This meeting has amply demonstrated that experimental
animals have a fundamental role to play in advancing our
understanding of intact organisms and the role that they play
in biomedical research. The concerns of our present-day
society--from hypertension, cancer, muscular dystrophy, and
cellular immunology to reproduction control, neurologic
disorders, etc.--represent a broad spectrum of problems that
demand a multidisciplinary approach and experimentation
requiring model animal systems. We have further heard at
this meeting that choice of the appropriate species and
planning of experimental designs involving numbers of animals
need careful attention. For most, if not all of the problems
mentioned above, the only appropriate vehicle for investigation at the moment is an animal model. The choice of animal
models for problems such as muscular dystrophy is indisput-
able. The public has the right to expect from the scientist
that the experimental design will ensure, as an overriding
principle, the greatest possible accuracy of the experimental
results. We have a right to expect that the accuracy of the
biological information received will lead to the highest
possible standards in implementation of knowledge.

We have heard calls for Congressional mandates for
alternative models to animal experimentation. Where appropriate, these are, of course, enthusiastically endorsed as
adding to our biological knowledge. However, we must be
careful that the American public is not deceived by mandating
models which are incapable of evaluating the fundamental
concerns that led to the support of the initial research
programs. Various computer models have been suggested. We
should be particularly attentive that these are thoroughly
tested before they are adopted.

As a microbiologist I am well aware of the opportunities
of understanding basic biological phenomena in single-cell
organisms. The Ames test for detecting potentially carcino-
genic compounds is a vivid recent demonstration of this
attempt. While I am proud that microbiology has made so many
important contributions to biology, it would be naive to
believe that an understanding of cell wall biosynthesis, DNA
replication, or macromolecular synthesis in Escherichia coli
has given us insights into more complex aspects of cancer,
such as cell-cell interactions, the function of the immune
system, and the role that nutrition and genetics play in
influencing susceptibility to cancer. Fundamental discoveries in biology made with simpler systems may ultimately have
to be retested with the intact animal. If we are going to be
true to our obligations, we have a responsibility to understand a biological principle at the molecular, cellular,
tissue, organismic, and societal level. It is critical that
basic biological principles be measured at various levels of

complexity. Only through such understandings can we discern those parameters that separate the bacteria from the fruit fly and from man itself. From recent studies on developmental biology, neurobiology, and related disciplines, it is clear that the impact of fundamental contributions made at the level of single cells must now be reexamined and reexplored in multicellular systems.

To carry out basic research one needs to have very bright people who are given freedom of action and have the opportunities to explore their own imagination. Lew Rosenstiel, in giving a grant to Brandeis, said, "Find the best people you can find, and then leave them alone." This is proper advice for management of basic science—as long as you add: Make sure they put in the correct overhead rate on their grant applications.

GENERATION OF PUBLIC POLICY

In the past few years there have been many intensive studies of science policy planning in which the scientific community was involved. President Ford instituted a Biomedical Research Panel. During the early part of the Carter administration the then Secretary of the Department of Health, Education and Welfare, Joseph Califano, conducted a similar policy study. The Congress held hearings on the Enabling Act for the National Science Foundation and recently on the use of animals in research. The list goes on. All of these studies recognized the need for programmatic contributions to society and the dependence of these on a strong basic science. What also emerges from these studies is a spectrum of scientific achievements that extends from unexpected findings arising from a series of highly motivated basic studies to their applications to a new technology.

Given this historical background of which there are many examples, one is led to the conclusion that in deciding science policy, committees should not be charged with generating initial research ideas. These will originate through the strong and healthy support of the basic science itself. What one must impose is a strict peer review process, so that the ideas under development are defensible, the new and basic information which is being gleaned is tested against some sort of fundamental basis for scientific knowledge, and animal experiments are conducted in appropriate numbers and in proper facilities. Improvements in the peer review system are required. The changes Dr. Malone suggested in this conference are timely and will resolve many of the outstanding problems. The editorial review process for our journals is a second tier of monitoring, which at the same time requires originality and diminishes unnecessary duplication.

In scientific laboratories the pressures of inflation and the limited financial resources available for research have put great pressures on experimental designs, including the use of experimental animals. There has been considerable motivation to replace animals with less expensive experimental systems whenever possible. The National Research Council, Institute of Laboratory Animal Resources, surveyed the use of animals in the decade 1968 to 1978. Last year they published their survey, showing that animal use declined by 40 percent during this time. This fact alone illustrates the continuing utilization of alternative procedures for research, education, and testing. There is no doubt that in the decade ahead alternatives to living animals will and should be employed whenever appropriate. The guiding principle, however, should be that the criterion of scientific excellence determines the experimental model to be used. These models cannot be mandated by law, but the public has a right to expect the highest possible confidence in the results of experiments employing animals.

Before one establishes interdisciplinary and cooperative groups to implement a given technology, there must be strict agreement as to the objectives, and all of the participants must agree that the probability of positive results is extremely high.

Another major point I would like to make is that there has been a great deal of discussion in Washington about the need for technology transfer. As a practicing scientist and observer of the scene, I am unaware of any significant body of scientific knowledge which is being held back by scientists from technologic utilization. In fact the pressures are exactly the reverse. The need for recognition, the desire to contribute to society's needs, and the wish to advance one's individual science are strong, compelling forces, which lead scientists to actively propose the uses of their science beyond their own basic research. Developing techniques and mechanisms to aid in technology transfer is indeed desirable, but I am unaware of any gap which currently exists that can be effectively filled by such mechanisms.

Many problems in modern society require scientific input. These include nuclear power, the use of waste products, nutrition, and better biomedical care and diagnosis. In discussions on science policy, the advice of scientists is frequently asked, and the public is then faced with a spectrum of comments to evaluate.

SOCIAL RESPONSIBILITY

The next responsibility on which I would like to comment
addresses itself to the scientist. Since the public is not
able to judge scientific competence, when a scientist speaks,
the question arises whether he or she is an authority on the
given topic or merely an expert in science itself. The
scientific community has a responsibility to monitor its
spokesmen to determine whether they are speaking on policy
issues in which they are uniquely knowledgeable. Given self-
constraints and proper public responsibility, the scientific
community does have a meaningful and responsive role to play
in determining public policy.

The individual scientist has a great opportunity to
contribute to this process through individual research
efforts, publications in scientific journals, and contributions to meetings on given topics. If one wishes to involve
oneself in the broader spectrum, opportunities abound to be
involved in study groups and advisory groups, to provide
advice to Congress, or to speak in the public media. In my
opinion, social responsibility requires that the individual
define his or her area of expertise when he or she speaks and
that he or she provide a balanced and reasonable discourse of
the facts available.

Scientific societies can play an important role in
shaping public policy and clarifying ethical considerations.
They can utilize specialists in their field to form a broad
consensus. On this basis they can respond to and inform the
executive, legislative, and judicial branches of government,
as well as respond to the public. I believe this is a proper
role for a professional society, as long as it speaks on the
basis of its scientific expertise, provides a balanced opportunity for the scientific issues to be debated, and assumes
responsibility for education and training. Scientists are
responsible for assisting the public and presenting all the
relevant facts and uncertainties. We should give serious
thought to the possibility that our existing scientific
institutions are not yet capable of evaluating the facts and
presenting them accurately to the public and that they are
not yet fully aware of their moral obligations. Ultimately,
the public must decide what risks (economic, environmental,
etc.) will be tolerated to achieve the expected benefits.

A COOPERATIVE APPROACH TO THE USE OF ANIMALS IN SCIENTIFIC
RESEARCH

With regard to this conference, public concern has been
expressed over the degree and amount of animal suffering that
can be justified for human benefit. Unquestionably, under
certain conditions our research animals are subjected to
painful procedures. We must do everything possible to minimize the number of such procedures and to insist on the use
of drugs to abrogate pain. In each case one must ask: Are
the societal stakes high enough to justify such experiments
with animals? This involves determining the benefits and
weighing them against the risks. Such ethical considerations
must involve the public, government, scientists, and scientific societies.

Public concern was clearly recognized in the passage of
the Laboratory Animal Welfare Act (Public Law 89-544) in
1966, marking a new era of research regulation. Subsequent
amendments in 1970 broadened this act to the current Animal
Welfare Act, which protects show horses, zoo and aquarium
species, and other categories of animals, as well as those
used in laboratories--but not pet dogs and cats and farm
animals. Current efforts to modify the Animal Welfare Act
should include expansion of the present coverage to include
pet dogs and cats and animals in municipal pounds or shelters
receiving Federal funds. The Endangered Species Conservation
Act of 1969, expanded to the Endangered Species Act of 1973,
responds to public concern regarding our ecosystems to pre-
serve endangered and threatened species.

RECOMMENDATIONS

This conference has identified a number of ways in which
the use and care of experimental animals can be improved. In
my opinion, there are two critical areas in which public
confidence in policies on the use of animals in research can
be increased: opening up the decision process to input from
an informed public, and expanding the training of personnel
dealing with animals.

We have several models of how the public can participate
in scientific ethical policy decisions. Some initially
involved public concerns that have significantly diminished
today. One involved the procedures developed to protect
human subjects in clinical studies in medical centers; another, the evaluation of guidelines for recombinant DNA
research. Lay representation participated in the Commission

on Human Subjects to establish a national consensus on guidelines for research on human subjects. This is now the responsibility of the President's Commission for the Study of
Ethical Practices in Biomedical and Social Research. All
clinical studies involving human subjects must be approved by
a local Human Subjects Committee, on which lay representatives also serve. The combined effect has been to broaden
the base of public input in an area of sensitive ethical
concerns, which ultimately also reinforced the research
goals. The public members served an important critical
function both at the national and local levels, and I believe
their participation was a significant factor in reassuring
the public that proper process and procedures were utilized.
Public members on the National Institutes of Health (NIH)
Advisory Committee for DNA Research and on the local Bio-
safety Committees have had a similar effect.

     In my opinion, it is timely to have a similar national
consensus for the care and use of laboratory animals. The
development of this consensus should include representatives
of the scientific community, the public, users of experimental animals, and organizations involved in production and
care of animals. The Guide for the Care and Use of Laboratory Animals, produced for NIH under the National Research
Council, as well as the Animal Care Assurance Statement
developed by the NIH, serve as a good starting point for
developing such a consensus. To be effective, the guidelines
must be national in scope and be overseen by institutional
committees which also contain members of the public. In the
last few years, recipients of NIH grants have been required
to submit an assurance statement; Federal funds can be with-
drawn for noncompliance, although this has happened only once
(6). In the light of experience, this system needs more
effective mechanisms for ensuring compliance, including
surveillance, on-site visits with trained peer-review teams,
and feedback to grant review committees. If the experiments
fail to meet guideline standards, the assurance statement
will lose its credibility.

     At the institutional level many mechanisms have been
suggested which can be applied. For example: (a) all proposals can be reviewed by the Animal Care Committee; (b) user
committees can be advisory and provide means for technicians,
graduate and postdoctoral students, faculty, and veterinarians to provide input, peer review, sensitivity to scientific
attitudes, and early warning; (c) the requirement for communication can be expanded to include internal publications,
open seminars, and contacts of well-informed scientists with
the public and news media; and (d) authority can be vested at

the highest institutional levels, with a coupled responsi- bility to inform the president, dean, etc., of the issues involved.

At the investigators' levels we must strive for kind-hand responsibility. Much of this cannot be regulated. For example, how do we responsibly determine stress and psycho- logical pain? If we were to answer honestly, it would be, "With difficulty." The development of a wide array of elec- trophysiological recording methods holds promise that quan- titative measurements may replace subjective judgments. Such efforts should be supported. At the same time, serious ethical problems exist involving the use of paralytic agents with operative procedures if concurrent anesthesia/analgesia is absent (such absence is forbidden by NIH rules) or unmonitored.

Critical to these deliberations is the question of pain, both acute and chronic. For acute pain the question could be asked: Is it sufficiently important to be tried first on humans? Study of a major human problem, chronic pain, is more difficult. It is hard to obtain suitable animal models, and the justification is more difficult. In such areas where the scientific design is less clear, yet a public health problem exists, we clearly need help in making decisions. I would suggest assembling a task force in which ethical as well as scientific expertise is used to explore or develop appropriate models.

Another area for improvement involves training of individuals working with experimental animals. Our greatest protection for quality experiments and for animals comes from training at all levels of personnel. As Dr. Edward Melby, Dean of the College of Veterinary Medicine, Cornell Univer- sity, pointed out at a recent House Subcommittee on Science, Research, and Technology hearing on Animals in Research (7): "Training programs have evolved in both the 2- and 4-year colleges to train animal technicians and technologists; a new specialty board was recognized by the American Veterinary Medical Association, and the American College of Laboratory Animal Medicine certifies veterinarians with advanced train- ing and experience in that specialty; and most institutions provide in-house training programs for animal technicians and graduate students, many following the programs fostered by the American Association for Laboratory Animal Science."

These nongovernmental agencies are to be applauded for their role in improving training. Better public understand- ing of their present activities is required, as well as a recognition by government and the public that the research projects themselves involve skills and theory in addition to work with animals. We need to broaden the base of training, including that of future scientists, and to make it more

available throughout the country, particularly in institutions that lack facilities for medical and veterinary
research. Professional societies should take the lead in
upgrading training.

Finally, we can exert control through our journals
without destroying the time-honored relationship between
author and editor. The opportunities are numerous, and a
number of examples have been suggested: (a) all journals
dealing with animals should be urged to publish the NIH
guidelines for research with animals; (b) authors could be
required to sign statements in submitting manuscripts that
these guidelines were followed; (c) in the review process,
the author, editor, and reviewer, each in turn, can be asked
to determine if these experiments follow the guidelines;
(d) the instructions to authors can be made more explicit,
requiring authors to supply more justification and more
detailed information on animal practices (since quality
science is served by the highest possible animal care, societal benefits would be maximized); (e) societies, where
journals are involved, should be encouraged to utilize their
ethics or animal committees to serve as review boards; and
(f) the Letters to the Editor column could be more effectively used to discuss and debate these issues.

CONCLUSIONS

The generous support of public funds to maintain an
extremely necessary venture in our society, the flow of basic
knowledge to technology, brings with it an added responsibility. Unless we understand this process and its limita-
tions, the determination of public policies will not be
appropriately achieved. Scientists must participate in any
process whereby major issues, such as the appropriate uses of
animals in research and teaching, are discussed. At this
conference we have begun.

REFERENCES

1. Barber, B., in "Conference on Social and Ethical
   Implications of Science and Technology," Institute for
   Research in Human Affairs, Graduate School and University
   Center of City University of New York, December 7-9
   (1977).
2. Sawhill, J. C., The role of science in higher education,
   Science 206, 281 (1979).

3. Bok, D., in "Annual Report to the Members of the Board of Overseers of Harvard University," pp. 11-12. Harvard University Press, Cambridge (1981).

4. Handler, P., Handler reflects on NAS, science issues, Chem. and Eng. News, p.20, Feb. 13 (1978).

5. Thomas, L., On the planning of science, in "Biochemical Scientists and Public Policy" (H. H. Fudenberg and V. L. Melnick, eds.), p. 67. Plenum Press, New York (1978).

6. Editorial, Scientist convicted for monkey neglect, Science 214, 1218 (1981).

7. Institute for Laboratory Animal Resource, National Academy of Sciences, "Animals in Research." National Academy Press, Washington, October 13-14 (1981).

SUMMARY OF RECOMMENDATIONS
ON ANIMAL EXPERIMENTATION

The major recommendations from the First Conference on
Scientific Perspectives in Animal Welfare organized by the
Scientists Center for Animal Welfare, November 11-13, 1981,
are detailed below. They are listed according to the
sequence of events rather than priority.

Inasmuch as there is general agreement that proper care
and use of experimental animals is desirable, it is recommended that:

1. Scientists must work continuously toward elimination or
prevention of unnecessary pain for research animals.
Discussions among scientists regarding currently acceptable practices should be encouraged. Investigators
should spend more time with their animals to improve
understanding of animal behavior and develop a sensitivity to their experimental animals. There is a need
to ensure that investigators understand the pathological
aspects and the behavioral, physiological, and other
essential requirements of the animals they use. Such
knowledge is necessary in order to preclude waste of
animals or financial resources, and to maximize scientific validity of experimental results.

2. Investigators discuss their research proposals with
other responsible scientists to obtain constructive
criticism of animal experimentation procedures before
submitting the protocol to the formal institutional
Animal Care and Use Committee for approval.

3. Institutional Animal Care and Use Committees include
members with a broad representation of viewpoints.
Inclusion of representation from animal and laboratory
technicians and graduate students was unanimously
endorsed. Community representatives and ethicists
should be invited to serve wherever local conditions
permit.

To be effective, the Committee must report directly
to the highest senior administrative officer of the
institution such as the President, or the Vice-President
for Research. The importance of strong administrative
support for the animal care program was emphasized. If
the administration is not truly supportive of the
program, investigators will be less motivated to pay
attention to such matters.

Furthermore, it is recommended that the institution's Supervisor of Animal Care or Director of the
Animal Facility may be a member of the Committee, but
not the Chairman. This would help assure credibility
with peers and the public. There was unanimous agreement on this point.

4. The public needs to be more aware of why and how
research is conducted on experimental animals. Scientists should maintain an "open-door" policy permitting
humane society representatives and the general public to
visit the laboratories and animal facilities. Young
people and school groups who visit by prior arrangement
should be welcomed. An open-door policy costs nothing
while a closed-door approach is no longer defensible and
may engender hostility.

5. Funding agencies require investigators applying for
grants to specifically address animal issues. Such
documentation would provide information to the reviewers
so that they can discharge their function of reviewing
proposals for proper treatment of animals.

6. Public and private funding agencies use consultants with
expertise in animal issues to review selected grant
proposals that present special concerns. Initially,
such consultants could serve as ad hoc review panel
members. Eventually, some funding organizations may
find it appropriate to establish entire committees
composed of such consultants, as has been done by the
Veterans Administration. In this system, review for
animal issues is performed by one committee and for
scientific merit by another.

7. Training courses be provided to scientists to increase
their empathy concerning the animals they are using, as
well as knowledge about established animal care policies. Such training could be particularly beneficial to
members and staff of review panels and institutional
Animal Care and Use Committees; to those who deal with
research involving primates, or endangered species; or

to those using highly invasive techniques on any animal species that is likely to cause severe or protracted pain (for instance, trauma or pain research). Such training would serve to enhance the effectiveness of peer pressure and the peer review system on which so much depends.

8. Accreditation of institutions by the American Association for the Accreditation of Laboratory Animal Care (AAALAC) be fostered. Currently, only 30 percent of research facilities in the United States are so accredited. As a first step, efforts should be made to see that all primate facilities achieve standards equivalent to AAALAC accreditation.

9. Inspection procedures by the Federal Government be improved. In 1981, the U.S. Department of Agriculture (USDA) promised changes in its inspection procedure for assessing compliance with the Animal Welfare Act. Also, in October 1981, the National Institutes of Health (NIH) promised to institute some site visits before issuing "Assurances" for compliance with NIH policies on animal care and use. Conference participants strongly endorsed this move and urged that it be done immediately. By April 1982, no site visits had taken place, but it is believed that some are being planned.

It was universally agreed that the present NIH Assurance Program for protection of research animals is ineffective. In contrast, the USDA inspection system can be and is working effectively in some locations. The effectiveness of this mechanism for improving and monitoring animal care is totally dependent on the competence and experience of the local inspector. Closer field supervision by regional directors and better training of veterinary medical officers was recommended.

10. "Codes of Practice" be established for all journals expressing editorial policy with reference to humane guidelines for animal care during experimentation. Topics to be addressed include use of analgesics, restraint procedures, and minimization of unnecessary pain, fear, anxiety, or deprivation. If papers do not meet the policy requirements, rejection with reasons will be given.

11. A journal editor's task of assessment for animal welfare measures would be enhanced by:

a. Each journal publishing guidelines for the welfare of experimental animals. This could be part of the section "Instructions to Authors" commonly published by many journals.

b. Stipulating that reviewers appraise submitted papers for compliance with appropriate animal welfare standards in addition to scientific merit.

c. Use of a numerical classification system for animal experimental procedures based on the degree of intervention and physical or psychological trauma to the animal. Such a system would help focus more attention on those manuscripts with a high degree invasive experimentation. Such a system is described by Professor K. J. Öbrink in this volume.

12. More funds be allocated by public and private sources for upgrading animal facilities. This could be done both through programs designed specifically for this purpose and as part of the construction and maintenance costs of regular research grants and contracts.

CONCLUSION

Given appropriate leadership and resources, the Scientists Center for Animal Welfare believes that support for most, if not all, of the above-listed recommendations would be forthcoming from the biomedical community. As a result, the quality of animal research would be enhanced and the accountability of scientists to the public would be improved.

ADDENDUM

The important topics of replacement of animals with other research methods and also the use of animals in teaching were beyond the scope of this conference program. This was the First Conference on Scientific Perspectives in Animal Welfare. It is hoped that additional recommendations specifically addressing these topics will emerge from future conferences in this series.

PARTICIPANTS

Perrie M. Adams, *Department of Psychiatry and Behavior Sciences, University of Texas Medical Branch, Galveston, Texas*

Ralph O. Anslow, *Litton Bionetics, Inc., Kensington, Maryland*

Henry J. Baker, *Department of Comparative Medicine, University of Alabama, Birmingham, Alabama*

Robert M. Berne, *Department of Physiology, University of Virginia School of Medicine, Charlottesville, Virginia*

Virginia Blair, *American Psychological Association, Washington, D.C.*

Sherman Bloom, *Department of Pathology, George Washington University Medical Center, Washington, D.C.*

Thomas H. Blosser, *The American Dairy Science Association, The American Society of Animal Science, and Beltsville Agricultural Research Center West, Beltsville, Maryland*

Edward J. Breyere, *Department of Biology, The American University, Washington, D.C.*

Leslie Bullock, *Department of Medicine, Hershey Medical Center, Hershey, Pennsylvania*

Tyler Burt, *Massachusetts General Hospital, Boston, Massachusetts*

Ansel Butterfield, *Bionetics, Inc., Hampton, Virginia*

Arthur B. Butterfield, *Animal Resources Facility, Georgetown University, Washington, D.C.*

Richard Carter, *Department of Pathology, University of North Carolina, Chapel Hill, North Carolina*

Helene Cecil, *Beltsville Agricultural Research Center East, U.S. Department of Agriculture, Beltsville, Maryland*

Leonard Cipriano, *General Electric and NASA Ames Research Center, Moffett Field, California*

Nancy Daunton, *Biomedical Research Division, NASA Ames Research Center, Moffett Field, California*

127

Donald Devincenzi, *NASA Headquarters, Washington, D.C.*

W. Jean Dodds, *Laboratories for Veterinary Science, New York State Department of Health, Albany, New York*

Ronald Dubner, *National Institute of Dental Research, National Institutes of Health, Bethesda, Maryland*

LeRoy Erickson, *McNeil Pharmaceutical, Spring House, Pennsylvania*

Carlos E. Eyzaguirre, *Department of Physiology, University of Utah College of Medicine, Salt Lake City, Utah*

Ronald E. Flatt, *Laboratory Animal Resources, Iowa State University, Ames, Iowa*

James W. Fleshman, *National Institute of Neurological and Communicative Disorders and Stroke, National Institutes of Health, Bethesda, Maryland*

Frank H. Flowers, *Canadian Council on Animal Care, Ottawa, Ontario, Canada*

James G. Fox, *Division of Comparative Medicine, Massachusetts Institute of Technology, Cambridge, Massachusetts*

Michael W. Fox, *Institute for the Study of Animal Problems, Washington, D.C.*

William I. Gay, *Division of Research Resources, National Institutes of Health, Bethesda, Maryland*

Frank B. Golley, *Institute of Ecology, University of Georgia, Athens, Georgia*

E. Gomersall, *NASA Ames Research Center, Moffett Field, California*

Janet C. Gonder, *Wisconsin Regional Primate Research Center, Madison, Wisconsin*

Thomas R. Griggs, *Department of Pathology, University of North Carolina, Chapel Hill, North Carolina*

Robert D. Gunnels, *Laboratory Animal Sciences Branch, Naval Medical Research Institute, Bethesda, Maryland*

Richard Halliwell, *Department of Medical Sciences, University of Florida College of Veterinary Medicine, Gainesville, Florida*

Harlyn O. Halvorson, *Rosenstiel Basic Medical Sciences Research Center, Brandeis University, Waltham, Massachusetts*

Judith E. Hampson, *Royal Society for Prevention of Cruelty to Animals, Horsham, West Sussex, England*

John E. Harkness, *Laboratory Animal Resources Department, Pennsylvania State University, University Park, Pennsylvania*

Richard A. Harris, *Animal Care Facility, U.S. Army Research Institute of Environmental Medicine, Needham, Massachusetts*

Thomas G. Hartsock, *Department of Animal Science, University of Maryland, College Park, Maryland*

James Harwell, *Veterinary Resources Branch, National Institutes of Health, Potomac, Maryland*

Angela B. Hefferman, *Canadian Federation of Humane Societies, Ottawa, Ontario, Canada*

Lee A. Heilman, *American Association for the Accreditation of Laboratory Animal Care (AAALAC), Joliet, Illinois*

Jack R. Hessler, *Animal Resource Division, University of Tennessee Center for the Health Sciences, Memphis, Tennessee*

Philip T. Johnson, *P. J. Associates, Chapel Hill, North Carolina*

Frederick W. L. Kerr, *Department of Neurologic Surgery, Mayo Foundation and Medical School, Rochester, Minnesota*

John D. Kessler, *Public Affairs, American Heart Association, Washington, D.C.*

D.R. Knauff, *Research Services, Wyeth Laboratories, Philadelphia, Pennsylvania*

Ernst Knobil, *Department of Physiology, University of Texas Medical School at Houston, Houston, Texas*

Keith Kraner, *Surgery, Anesthesiology and Trauma Study Section, National Institutes of Health, Bethesda, Maryland*

Robert J. Lee, *Flow Laboratories, Inc., McLean, Virginia*

Paul H. Lenz, *Office of Extramural Research and Training, Office of the Director, National Institutes of Health, Bethesda, Maryland*

David Lewis, *Clinical Research Center, University of Linköping, Linköping, Sweden*

Leon L. Lewis, *Laboratory of Animal Resources, Department of Laboratory Animal Resources, Hoffman–LaRoche, Nutley, New Jersey*

William G. Lillis, *Berlex Laboratories, Cedar Knolls, New Jersey*

Franklin M. Loew,[1] *Division of Comparative Medicine, The Johns Hopkins University, Baltimore, Maryland*

Chaman Malhan, *Laboratory of Animal Facilities, New York University Medical Center, New York, New York*

Thomas E. Malone, *Office of the Director, National Institutes of Health, Bethesda, Maryland*

Arnett Matchett, *Animal Medicine and Technology, U.S. Department of Agriculture, Animal Care Staff, Hyattsville, Maryland*

James D. McGrady, *Department of Veterinary Physiology and Pharmacology, College of Veterinary Medicine, Texas A&M University, College Station, Texas*

Joan McIntosh, *National Institute of Neurological and Communicative Disorders and Stroke, National Institutes of Health, Bethesda, Maryland*

Paul E. Meckley, *Laboratory Animal Care, Department of Animal Science, University of Delaware, Newark, Delaware*

Wellington Moore, *Laboratory Animal Health, Auburn University School of Veterinary Medicine, Auburn, Alabama*

J. Moor-Jankowski, *LEMSIP, New York University Medical School, New York, New York*

Albert E. New, *Laboratory Animal Science, National Cancer Institute, National Institutes of Health, Bethesda, Maryland*

Karl J. Öbrink, *Department of Physiology, Uppsala University, Uppsala, Sweden*

[1]Present address: *Dean, School of Veterinary Medicine, Tufts University, Boston, Massachusetts.*

F. Barbara Orlans, *National Heart, Lung, and Blood Institute, National Institutes of Health, Bethesda, Maryland*

Amos E. Palmer, *National Cancer Institute, National Institutes of Health, Frederick Cancer Research Center, Frederick, Maryland*

Joseph E. Pierce, *Laboratory Animal Medicine and Surgery Section, National Heart, Lung, and Blood Institute, National Institutes of Health, Vienna, Virginia*

Fred Quimby, *Department of Pathology, Cornell University Medical College, New York, New York*

David J. Ramsay, *Department of Physiology, University of California School of Medicine, San Francisco, California*

Susan Reardon, *College of Veterinary Medicine, Michigan State University, East Lansing, Michigan*

Orr E. Reynolds, *American Physiological Society, Bethesda, Maryland*

Clifford Roberts, *Rockville Maryland*

Margaret Rose, *University of New South Wales School of Surgery, and Australian Veterinary Association, Kensington, Australia*

Sheila Rosenthal, *Environmental Protection Agency, Washington, D.C.*

Andrew Rowan, *The Institute for the Study of Animal Problems, Washington, D.C.*

Harry C. Rowsell, *Canadian Council on Animal Care, and Department of Pathology, University of Ottawa, Ottawa, Ontario, Canada*

Robert I. Russell, *National Naval Medical Center, Bethesda, Maryland*

Lilly-Marlene Russow, *Department of Philosophy, Purdue University, West Lafayette, Indiana*

Harold Sandler, *Biomedical Research Division, NASA Ames Research Center, Moffett Field, California*

Ann Marie Serwa, *Microbiological Associates, Bethesda, Maryland*

Richard C. Simmonds, *Department of Laboratory Animal Medicine, Uniformed Services University of the Health Sciences, Bethesda, Maryland*

Gerald D. Smith, *Laboratory Animal Resources, School of Veterinary Medicine, Louisiana State University, Baton Rouge, Louisiana*

Orland Soave, *Interagency Primate Steering Committee, National Institutes of Health, Bethesda, Maryland*

Sheldon Steinberg, *School of Veterinary Medicine, University of Pennsylvania, Philadelphia, Pennsylvania*

James F. Taylor, *U.S. Army Medical Research and Development Command, Fort Detrick, Frederick, Maryland*

Garth J. Thomas, *Center for Brain Research, University of Rochester Medical Center, Rochester, New York*

Mildred S. Warfield, *National Institute of Allergy and Infectious Diseases, National Institutes of Health, Bethesda, Maryland*

Marc E. Weksler, *Department of Medicine, Cornell University Medical College, New York, New York*

Robert A. Whitney, Jr., *Veterinary Resources Branch, Division of Research Services, National Institutes of Health, Bethesda, Maryland*
James A. Will, *Research Animal Resources Center, The University of Wisconsin, Madison, Wisconsin*
Thomas Wolfle, *Veterinary Resources Branch, Division of Research Services, National Institutes of Health, Bethesda, Maryland*
Eugene M. Wright, Jr., *Department of Comparative Medicine, University of Virginia, Charlottesville, Virginia*